Who Knows the Colour of God?

Breaking Open the Word

Who Knows the Colour of God?

Homilies and Reflections
for Year C

Corbin Eddy

© 2000 Novalis, Saint Paul University, Ottawa, Canada

Cover: Blair Turner

Layout: Gilles Lepine

Business Office:
Novalis
49 Front Street East, 2nd Floor
Toronto, Ontario, Canada
M5E 1B3

Phone: 1-800-387-7164 or (416) 363-3303
Fax: 1-800-204-4140 or (416) 363-9409
E-mail: novalis@interlog.com

Canadian Cataloguing in Publication Data

Eddy, Corbin, 1942–

    Who knows the colour of God?

(Breaking open the Word; 3)

ISBN 2-89507-045-8

    1. Church year sermons. 2. Sermons, Canadian (English).
3. Catholic Church – sermons. 4. Bible. N.T. Luke – Sermons.
I. Title. II. Series.

BX1756.E36 2000   252'.6   C00-901332-6

Printed in Canada.

We acknowledge the financial support of the Government of Canada through the Book Publishing Industry Development Program (BPIDP) for our publishing activities.

NOVALIS

Table of Contents

to the people of
St. Basil's Parish,
Ottawa

Introduction

The person who preaches in the context of the liturgical
assembly is a mediator, representing both the community and
the Lord. The assembly gathers for liturgy as a community of
faith, believing that God has acted in human history and more
particularly, in their own history. The community gathers to
respond to this living and active God. They may also gather
to question how or whether God who once acted in human
history is still present and acting today.... The preacher represents this community by voicing its concerns, by naming its
demons, and thus enabling it to gain some understanding and
control of the evil which afflicts it. The preacher represents
the Lord by offering the community another word, a word of
healing and pardon, of acceptance and love.

Bishops' Committee on Priestly Life and Ministry,
Fulfilled in Your Hearing
(Washington: USCC, 1982), 6.

More than writing biographies of Jesus or strictly historical
accounts of his life and times, the evangelists were involved in the
homiletic enterprise. The life, death and resurrection of Jesus was their
text. Each of them sought in their own time to be creative, to reflect
and communicate a particular approach to the person and ministry of
Jesus that they believed would work for their own communities.

The preoccupations of each gospel reflect the living experience of
living communities for whom the Risen Christ is proclaimed as source
of healing, pardon, acceptance and liberation. That there are four of
them is already an invitation for preachers and teachers to "Go and do
likewise," to discern what is happening in the worlds of their

communities and to creatively address what is happening with gospel words of hope and promise.

In preparing to preach, I am struck over and over again by three things: how pertinent and perennial the issues are which the scriptures raise, how artfully and enticingly their authors raise them, and how engaging these ancient texts can be as conversation partners for our own time. The role of the homilist is to facilitate the assembly's discovery or rediscovery of the texts in all three ways: to recognize and face the issue at hand, to understand and appreciate the author's approach to the issue, and to engage the assembly in the conversation.

Within a liturgical context, the homilist has the further mission to draw the assembly through the word into communion with each other and with God, a communion that will be sealed in the eucharist. The many facets of dying and rising that the scriptures proclaim point ultimately to the person of Jesus in whom believers are called to become "one bread, one body." It is my experience that approaching the preaching ministry in this way has been fascinating and life-giving, both for me personally and for the communities I've been privileged to serve as pastor.*

The gospel of Luke provides the centrepiece for the lectionary of Year C. Frederick Danker, in his brief introduction to the gospel for preachers (*Luke: Proclamation Commentaries Series,* Philadelphia: Fortress Press, 1976) notes that none of the issues Luke faced was more daunting or challenging for him than the parochial concepts of God which penetrated the Mediterranean world of his time. Fixed theological ideas and inherited cultic habits were difficult to overcome. They die hard. Prospective converts to Christianity from both the Jewish Diaspora and the non-Jewish world, comfortable with their own cultures, set traditions and rules, seem to have "gotten Luke's goat." Luke's Jesus is very hard on a God that's too small, a worldview that's too comfortable, or a community that's too set in its patterns of thought and behaviour. He tackles these issues head on.

---

* For further reflection on "conversation," I would recommend James B.Dunning, *Echoing God's Word* (Arlington VA: North American Forum on the Catechumenate, 1993).

By chance this summer, I happened to hear a delightful interview on CNN with Mark Caldwell. He had just published *A Short History of Rudeness*, and was commenting on the difference "in-your-face directness" has made in the course of history, and how a certain politeness and sensitivity to the feelings of others can be an obstacle to truth and life. He illustrated his point with the famous parable of the child who finally jumped up and said, "The emperor has no clothes," as the others tried to pretend that their naked monarch was fully and magnificently attired.

Jesus, as Luke presents him, functions "in your face." He tells it like it is, especially if he thinks religious faith and practice are choking people, or stifling communication, understanding and growth. Sometimes he's even a bit rude, but more often offers a metaphor, parable or healing, the point of which can't be missed. His gospel is filled with surprises, paradoxes and reversals (and sometimes rude awakenings) such as the Good Samaritan, the Pharisee and Publican, the Prodigal Son, and the Rich Man and Lazarus, to highlight very dramatic parables that are unique to his gospel. Jesus' healings of the centurion's son and the ten lepers, and the raising of the son of the widow of Naim propose similar awakenings. What is God really like? What is God doing in the world? How should humans think about God and pray to God? In light of the kingdom of God, which Jesus proclaims, how do humans think about, relate with and serve each other?

The keynote is sounded right at the beginning. Luke introduces Jesus' public ministry with a liturgy of the word. First the scripture is read.

> The spirit of the Lord is upon me, because he has anointed me to bring good news to the poor. He has sent me to proclaim release to the captives and recovery of sight to the blind, to let the oppressed go free, to proclaim the year of the Lord's favour.

Scroll rolled up, Jesus' homily follows. "Today this scripture has been fulfilled in your hearing."

The agenda is clear. God in Jesus is about big "people issues": good news for the poor, release, vision, freedom and grace. What is unique to Luke is his second volume, the Acts of the Apostles, which parallels the gospel in its conviction that the work of the church mirrors that of Jesus, an ongoing challenge to the church in every age. We too are to be about big people issues.*

These homilies were not originally intended for publication, but were preached Sunday after Sunday at St. Basil's Church in Ottawa, Ontario, where I was pastor for eight years. Ron Warren, who served on the pastoral council, began taping them, especially for use among parishioners who were unable to get to Mass regularly. The tapes were stored in the parish library, and were occasionally borrowed by parishioners who wanted to hear a particular homily again or share it with a friend. When Bernadette Gasslein moved to Ottawa and joined St. Basil's, she discovered the tapes and encouraged me to make them available to a wider public. Michelle Rocheleau transcribed them, and now, *finally*, one full year of homilies has been reconstructed and revised in this form. I am grateful to Ron, Michelle and Bernadette for pushing and prodding me in this direction. Bernadette Gasslein subsequently took on the task of editing them for publication, and I want to thank her especially for her skill and patience. I want to thank as well the parishioners of St. Basil's for their attentive and active listening, for their many comments and questions, for engaging in the conversation.

Even in their present form, however, their style and content is *oral*. They are conversational. They presume that the texts have been proclaimed, that there have been significant silences between them, and that the assembly is ready to be engaged in the conversation, the "table talk" which will move them forward to the eucharist.

Walter Brueggemann has a wonderful way of describing what I have tried to do, however modestly, in these homilies.

> Poets, in the moment of preaching, are permitted to perceive and voice the world differently, to dare a new phrase, a new picture, a free juxtaposition of matters long known. Poets are authorized to invite a new conversation, with new voices

---

* For an excellent commentary for preachers on Luke-Acts, I would recommend: Luke Timothy Johnson, *The Gospel of Luke* (Collegeville: Liturgical Press-Glazier, 1991) and Luke Timothy Johnson, *The Acts of the Apostles* (Collegeville: Liturgical Press-Glazier, 1992).

sounded, new hearings possible. The new conversation may end in freedom to trust and courage to relinquish. The new conversation, on which our very lives depend, requires a poet and not a moralist. Because, finally, church people are like other people, we are not changed by new rules. The deep places in our lives—places of resistance and embrace—are not ultimately reached by instruction. Those places of resistance and embrace are reached only by stories, images, metaphors and phrases that line out the world differently, apart from our fear and hurt.

Walter Brueggemann, *Finally Comes the Poet*
(Minneapolis: Fortress Press, 1989), 109-110.

Finally: *Who Knows the Colour of God?* A propos of the title, let me conclude with this:

Kevin was in Grade 1 at school. His teacher asked the class, "What is the colour of apples?" Most of the children answered red. A few said green. Kevin raised his hand and said white. The teacher tried to explain that apples could be red, green or sometimes golden, but never white. Kevin was quite insistent and finally said, "Look inside."

I think that Luke would like Kevin—a lot!

Corbin Eddy
Saint Mary's Seminary and University
Baltimore, MD
Feast of St. Augustine
August 28, 2000

Discriminating Watchfulness

First Sunday of Advent

Jeremiah 33.14-16
Psalm 25
1 Thessalonians 3.12-4.2
Luke 21.25-28, 34-36

As unrealistic as it might sound, the liturgy of Advent invites sober, discriminating watchfulness and careful discernment—in a month which for many of us is filled with family and social customs and obligations, office parties, end of semester examinations, perhaps even a financial house to be put in order before the calendar flips over to a new year. All too often preachers moan and groan about secularization, the consumer rush of Christmas, the "death" of Advent. Let's try something else.

The November 1997 issue of *National Geographic* presented a beautiful preview of an upcoming book of photographs called *Chased by the Light*. For ninety days one year, from the autumnal equinox to the winter solstice, the usually travelling photographer Jim Brandenburg stayed put at his home, which he describes as a "wild isolated place outside the small, end-of-the-road town of Ely, Minnesota."

"I had set myself the challenge," he writes, "that for ninety days between the autumnal equinox and winter solstice I would take only one photograph a day. There would be no second exposure, no second chance. My work would be stripped to the bone and rely on whatever photographic and woods skills I have."

As a professional photographer, Brandenburg had become accustomed to being in situations where he would take up to five hundred pictures a day. Just do it—shoot—and choose later. During these ninety days of increasing darkness, in the familiar surroundings of his own home territory, he was going to do something different. He would spend the whole day seeking out *one* opportunity for *one* photograph. During these ninety days it would be a question of discipline and focus.

"Am I an artist," he was asking himself, "or do I just take so many pictures that I will somehow 'luck out'?" Do I have a discriminating and critical eye? Each photograph in this book must be a true original, like a painting—not the best selected from rolls and rolls of similar frames. He saw himself like Henry David Thoreau, who had gone into the woods of New England because he "wished to live deliberately, to confront only the essential facts of life—to transact some private business with the fewest obstacles—to anticipate not the sunrise and the dawn merely, but, if possible, Nature herself."

Today's gospel text from Luke holds out an invitation similar to that which nature offered to Brandenburg and Thoreau before him. It is an invitation from Jesus to discriminating watchfulness—"waiting in hope."

Waiting for the end times—or for the judgment—is looking ahead to that fullness of time when God in Christ will finally and completely clarify what life at its core is all about: what is the very essence of life, what matters and what does not. He invites his hearers to consider their present life and experience in light of and from the perspective of that last day. What will today look like from that vantage point? What will this December look like from that vantage point?

In the *New Revised Standard Version* translation, Luke's gospel quotes Jesus as saying: "Be on guard so that your hearts are not weighed down with dissipation and drunkenness and the worries of this life, and that day catch you unexpectedly, like a trap." (Luke 21.34-35a) The *New American Bible* translation uses the word "bloated" instead of "weighed down."

I'm sure that all of us could tell stories flowing out of these images. Who doesn't know something about the "dissipation" of being pulled here and there, to and fro? Who hasn't felt a kind of "drunken stupor" when life seems nothing but an unreal blur? Who hasn't felt "weighed down" or "bloated" with the cares and concerns of life, big and small?

The same Greek word found in today's gospel which we translate as "weighed down or bloated" recurs in the account of the transfiguration of Jesus where, although their eyes were "weighed down," the disciples Peter, James and John stayed awake and saw his glory.

It occurs again in Matthew's telling of Jesus' agony in the garden. The eyes of the disciples were "heavy" and, in this case, they fell asleep. Here the word hints at a kind of depression. "Maybe if I just go to sleep, everything will be better when I wake up." Did you ever have that feeling? Being watchful, vigilant and in touch with reality isn't always easy.

Many of us may never have the opportunity to go to the woods to "transact our private business with the fewest obstacles" or to study the scene so carefully that our picture of it is "right."

However, even in the midst of the pressured busy-ness that many of us feel, we do want and *need* to hear the liturgy's Advent invitation to discriminating watchfulness and vigilance. In our heart of hearts we all want to see life clearly and get the picture.

Might I suggest that we centre our prayer this week on the first verse of the psalm appointed for today: "Make me know your ways, O Lord; teach me your paths. Lead me in your truth, and teach me, for you are the God of my salvation." (Psalm 25.4–5a)

When the Valleys Fill Up and the Mountains Fall Down

Second Sunday of Advent

Baruch 5.1-9
Psalm 126
Philippians 1.3-6, 8-11
Luke 3.1-6

For God has ordered that every high mountain and the ever-lasting hills be made low, and the valleys filled up, to make level ground, so that Israel may walk safely in the glory of God. (Baruch 5.7)

The tense longing of weary exiles. People walking without the benefit of the shoes and gear that we have for hiking today. People walking towards an unknown future, an unknown location, with everything they own on their backs. All they know is that they're fleeing danger and death.

That kind of experience is probably very remote for most of us, although we may well have heard stories from our parents or grand-parents about attempted escapes over the Berlin wall. We may know someone who lived through a train wreck and had to climb through a window and run because the car might blow up. Or think of how frightened people must have been when they have had to flee their sinking, overloaded ferries into the open sea. They knew the danger that lay behind them. Where they were going, what was going to happen to them, about that, they were very unclear. They just knew that they had to go.

Even though there have been mass movements of refugees in our own century, most of us have not been personally involved in them. Some of us may have been touched in a very important way through Project 4000, which was so interesting and so successful. We might know some of the large numbers of Cambodian refugees who settled here in Ottawa because of its efforts; we might therefore know their stories. But these images of mountains levelling out before us and valleys being filled as we see our destiny and the possibility for some kind of security, serenity or home, probably don't touch us as they would have touched the persons to whom they were originally directed.

In the gospel text, the images change. They no longer deal with the need to escape from physical danger and harm. Here the images deal with a more spiritual, inner experience. John the Baptist uses those images to speak not of a mass movement of exiles, but of a personal movement into the waters of the Jordan for forgiveness of sins, reconciliation and healing. His is an invitation to move away from a danger or peril that we experience within ourselves to fuller and more abundant life.

Imagine the mountains moving and the valleys being filled as a person moves from the bottle to serenity, or the mountains that have to open up as a person who is trapped by drugs rebuilds their life. Think of the mountains and obstacles that someone who faces life-threatening illness has to deal with: the peril that such a person experiences, not only in their body, but also in their spirit. Anyone who has a disease has to endure a similar movement. Imagine the journey that a person must make when their husband or wife dies, or when their young child dies suddenly or takes their own life. The obstacles, the mountains, the valleys they face, as they try to find some serenity, some meaning, some potential for newness and peace.

John is inviting people to look to God for this newness, to go to the Jordan, the same river through which the Hebrew exiles passed years ago under Joshua's leadership. They found their home on their own side of the Jordan. The waters opened up for them twice: first, the Sea of Reeds or the Red Sea opened as Moses led the people; then the Jordan River, where Joshua led them. John is saying that as, in our own interior journey, we come to understand whatever might enslave us, we can go back into the Jordan and come out purified, refreshed and renewed. God's Spirit offers this possibility to us.

In one of his books, Rabbi Harold Kushner relates these images to Murphy's law and the law of God proclaimed by the prophets. Murphy's law: whatever can go wrong, will go wrong. God's law: whatever can be made right could be made right. Whatever can be made right, could be made right. Healing, reconciliation, new beginnings, life, serenity: go down to the Jordan and up you come with new possibilities for yourself, your family, your community.

Exile isn't just the physical experience of the Israelites long ago, or of today's refugees who wait to find a country to receive them. There are other ways of being distant from a safe harbour. There are other ways of being distant from serenity and from a real home. Standing at the edge of the Jordan, John the Baptist invites us to be in deeper contact with those places of exile in our own lives. He urges us to be open to the possibility of mountains being levelled and valleys filled up as we move ahead. The experience of exile isn't the experience of every human being, but what John is talking about belongs to us all. The challenge is to name it, claim it and move with it.

Give Your Cloak to the Roses of Winter

Third Sunday of Advent

Zephaniah 3.14–18a
Isaiah 12
Philippians 4.4–7
Luke 3.10–18

Sing aloud, O daughter Zion; shout, O Israel! Rejoice and exult with all your heart, O daughter Jerusalem! The Lord has taken away the judgments against you, he has turned away your enemies. The king of Israel, the Lord, is in your midst; you shall fear disaster no more. (Zephaniah 3.14–15)

Whoever has two coats must share with anyone who has none; and whoever has food must do likewise. (Luke 3.11)

At first sight, these texts really don't seem to go together—to be honest they probably don't—but since the liturgy one Friday at Saint John's, Collegeville, when I was on sabbatical, they have come together for me. We were celebrating the December 12 Feast of Our Lady of Guadalupe, Patroness of the Americas, the day on which the Synod of the Americas was completing its work in Rome. The homilist at Mass told the story behind the feast. I had known its broad outline, but hadn't really thought much about it.

As children we learned that Columbus "discovered" America in 1492. We are often reminded, however, by native Americans of both the southern and northern hemispheres, that America was here long before Columbus "discovered" it and that the arrival of European explorers, missionaries, yes, and conquerors, too, was a mixed blessing for the land and for its peoples. For those of us who trace our origins to European ancestors, these reminders were especially conscience troubling in 1992 as we celebrated the 500th anniversary of our arrival here.

The scene is 1531, only thirty-nine years after Columbus landed. The traditional Aztec culture and religion of what is now Mexico is already virtually destroyed, at least in its external and public manifestations.

Juan Diego, a young Indian convert to Christianity, was passing by the ruins of an Aztec temple at Tepeyac, a hill northwest of Mexico City. It was there that he had an experience of God in the person of Mary. She asked him, "Where are you going?" When he didn't answer, she instructed him to go to the bishop to suggest that a church be built on that very spot. The bishop, as might be expected, did not take him very seriously.

Three days later, he was still "going"—actually he was busy looking after an uncle who was ill. Mary appeared to him again, this time on the road—the story goes that Juan's uncle was cured at that moment—and told him to pick the roses that were growing on the hill and bring them to the bishop as a sign that she was serious. It was not the season for roses, and they wouldn't grow on that hill anyway, but there they were. He picked them, rolled them up in his poncho (designed very much like the chasuble I'm wearing) and brought them to the bishop.

They say that this coat or cloak served not only as protection during the day but could be reconfigured as a pup tent at night. It was a very important part of Juan's life.

When the bishop received him, Juan opened this coat. The roses fell to the floor, and on his "chasuble" was a remarkable picture of Mary that continues to be a central treasure of the Mexican people, and a challenge to the "Americas."

She is crowned, standing on a crescent moon, supported by an angel. She stands in front of the sun, and is clothed with a star-studded sky.

The gods of the Aztecs are well represented, as is the Christian Book of Revelation. Clothed with the stars, she stands on the moon and in front of the sun, signifying that she is affirming natural religious traditions, but is somehow their superior. Wearing a crown, she relativizes imperial power. With eyes downcast, she humbly declares that she is not a god. With folded hands, her image speaks of gentle prayerfulness. With a skin tone and facial features not really black, brown, olive, or white, she signals universality. With a hint of being pregnant, she heralds a new world and a fresh start for everyone. Looking remarkably like ancient Christian icons, she speaks Nahuatl, the language of the Aztecs.

"Where are you going?" she asks, and when the youthful Juan Diego stops to wonder, there roses are growing. When he offers his coat to the roses, a marvellous icon is given in return. Even now it continues to invite hope for a world yet unborn, a world where God's daughter Zion, the capital city of all people, is called to rejoice, and where judgments against the poor can be overturned. Surrounded, supported by and wearing the symbols of divinity, the Lady of Guadalupe is an icon of promise—an icon of universal and motherly dominion that speaks the language of a conquered people and asks them to take seriously the direction of their lives.

The fact that bishops and popes have laid a claim to her and named her "Patroness of New Spain," "Queen of Mexico" or "Empress of the Americas" has not taken her away from the poor and from others who think they have nothing to lose by offering their coat to the roses of winter.

The pregnant Lady of Advent—the joyful, hopeful daughter of Zion—continues to be an icon of hope and promise for all who are ready to be challenged with her penetrating question: "Where are you going?"

Zephaniah, John the Baptist and Paul in his letter to the Philippians ask the same basic kinds of questions about our own sense of direction; the wonderful story of Juan Diego and his experience of the Lady of Guadalupe echoes them.

"Do not fear; do not let your hands grow weak; the Lord, your God is in your midst ... to renew you in his love." "Let your gentleness be known to everyone. The Lord is near." "Give your coat to the roses of winter and see what can happen to your vision of the world."

Who Knows the Colour of God?

Fourth Sunday of Advent

Micah 5.2–5
Psalm 80
Hebrews 10.5–10
Luke 1.39–45

Elizabeth was the wife of Zechariah, the priest. Today we would call them both senior citizens. Her time for bearing children was long past. Zechariah probably had the opportunity to offer incense at the altar of the Lord two or three times in his whole career, since the priests would take turns doing that. Now, at the very privileged moment when Zechariah is offering the incense, a heavenly visitor tells him that his wife Elizabeth will bear a son. With all of his knowledge of the tradition, all of his sophistication, Zechariah should have been expected to recognize and honour the angel's presence. Instead, Zechariah wavers. Nevertheless, Elizabeth is with child. A wonder, a miracle, a divine intervention points to the very special and privileged place that Elizabeth's son will have in God's plan. Her situation is not entirely without precedent. We know well the story of those other senior citizens, Abraham and Sarah. Remember Sarah's response when God visited them, announcing that she would be with child, the mother of a multitude of nations, no less? She laughed. Why? We're not sure. You've probably caught yourself laughing just out of nervousness—an inappropriate response: you don't know what to do, so you laugh. Perhaps it was that simple. She might have been laughing out of joy. She might have been laughing at the visitor because the news was so preposterous. But Sarah laughs, and Sarah becomes Isaac's mother.

Another story, less familiar but equally interesting and wonderful, is found in the thirteenth chapter of the Book of Judges. The Israelites, who had been seized by the Philistines, had been in captivity for forty years when a visitor, an angel, came to the barren wife of Menoa. (Only her husband is named in the story.) The angel announced that the woman was going to have a son and gave her the advice that people give expectant mothers, even today: don't drink anything strong, don't do anything crazy, get lots of rest, watch your diet. The angel gives this advice and leaves. Menoa's wife talks to her husband about this heavenly visitor, but Menoa doesn't believe her. He responds, "If an angel is coming, let the angel come to *me*. You go about your own business with your crazy dreams." The angel comes back. Menoa's wife runs to get her husband. Menoa goes to meet the angel and says, "If this child is going to be a miracle baby, there must be a reason. He must have a special place in God's plan. What am I going to do? How am I going to train him? How am I going to get ready for his birth? What will I have to do to make sure that he turns out as God wants him to turn out?"

The angel gives both father and mother very good advice: pray a lot, worry not at all, because your child's life will unfold. They have that kind of inner freedom. The father wants the angel to stay for supper. He wants to know the angel's name. He wants to know what's going to be expected of the child. The angel disappears. The angel gave another order, however: the young boy was never to have a razor touch him. He was to let his hair and his beard grow. He was to be natural—a *nazarite*. In his gospel, Matthew emphasizes that Jesus was from Nazareth to connect Jesus and Samson, the son of Menoa, who loses his strength as soon as he cuts his hair.

These are the wonderful stories of barren wives giving birth to children who play key roles in God's plan as it unfolds: Isaac, Samson, John the Baptist. In Mary's story is something absolutely unprecedented. Mary's baby has no earthly father. Abraham, Menoa and Zechariah, old as they are, are named and they are real. What happens to Mary has no precedent. Luke is not concerned about biology when he insists on her virginity. His concern is theological, mystical and spiritual.

One day on his CBC radio show, *Gilmour's Albums,* Clyde Gilmour played a song that was written by Oscar Brand. Brand grew up in Winnipeg and now lives in New York, where he is a prominent musician and choir leader. The song is found on an album that was issued in 1980; as with so many of the things Gilmour talks about, it's out of print. I hadn't heard this song before, but it would be wonderful with children's choirs. It starts with Mary fussing. "What colour is my son going to be?" she asks, because she doesn't know what colour his father is. "What's he going to look like? What is the shape of his eyes going to be because I don't know what colour God is?" The next verse has Joseph worrying. "It's going to be very, very clear that he's not going to look like me because I'm not his father. What is he going to look like? And is everybody going to know, just looking at him, that he's not mine? What is he going to look like?" The chorus, which is sung by the children, goes, "Who knows the colour of God? Black or white or yellow or red, all or any or none of the above. Who knows the colour of God knows the colour of love." Jesus, the son of David? Yes and no. Joseph is the son of David. Jesus isn't Joseph's son. Jesus an Israelite? Yes and no, but more than an Israelite. Jesus, the fulfillment of the ancient Hebrew prophecies? Yes and no. Yes and no. He is more than anything that they could have hoped for, because Jesus, the son of God, is everyone's brother. This insight has been manifested in the history of Christian art, where Jesus has appeared with every possible skin tone, every possible hairstyle, every possible eye shape. Why? Because Jesus is bigger than anything that we can name or picture. The colour of Jesus is the colour of love. The shape of Jesus' eyes is the shape of love.

If Jesus fulfills any of the Old Testament prophecies or any of the Old Testament expectations fully, it's that of Isaiah 56. Isaiah noted that foreigners who come to Israel are really never fully and finally at home. Isaiah admonishes the people: "Make sure that no stranger among you could ever say one day that the Lord could separate me from his real people. Never let strangers feel that they are just being tolerated or they aren't really a part of who you are. Let them join themselves to the Lord. Let them minister to God. Let them love God's name. Let them serve God. Let them keep the Sabbath. Let them hold fast to the covenant. Let them be led to the holy mountain to be joyful in my house of prayer."

God admonished the Hebrews long ago through the prophet Isaiah. In the person of Jesus, God admonishes us today in the virgin birth. The mystery of the virgin birth, far from distancing Jesus from other humans, links us to him. Because Jesus is the son of God, he is the brother of all people. The mystery of the virgin birth invites all of us to be different kinds of people in the light of Jesus, whose colour is love and whose eyes are love-shaped.

God Rest Ye Merry

Christmas Day

Isaiah 52.7-10
Psalm 98
Hebrews 1.1-6
John 1.1-18

I'm sure that you all have seen the beautiful photograph of our fragile-looking blue planet taken from space very early in the history of space exploration. If I'm not mistaken, it was taken in July 1969 when Neil Armstrong and his two fellow astronauts landed on the moon. Once again, if I remember correctly, they said something like this as they looked back at the earth: "We see the earth as it truly is, small and blue and beautiful, floating in the silence. To see the earth from this distance invites us to recognize ourselves and all people as fellow travellers, truly brothers and sisters."

The same photograph was used more recently in a short television piece, accompanied by Bette Midler's popular song "[God is watching] From a Distance." The moral or lesson to be learned from the intersection of the song and the photograph seemed to be that, because God is watching, we need to be working hard at protecting both the planet and our relationships with one another. Because God is watching, we need to be building peace. It may also have been an invitation to imagine ourselves looking down at the world from God's perspective and seeing how the earth is one, fragile, clearly to be shared by all the forms of life which it sustains, and protected by the human race.

As interesting and powerful as those images and connections might be, Christmas puts a very different spin on the world, and on the relationship of the world with God. The Christmas Feast does not image God as watching from a distance but as personally involved in the life of the world. God's not "up there" but *on* the planet, directly and personally involved in all the messiness of building "peace on earth, good will among people."

To illustrate this contrasting theological perspective, I'd like to suggest that you picture our fragile blue earth once again. As you do so, hear the first verse of another popular song—a Christmas carol. You may wish to sing it, but make sure you keep the picture of earth in mind.

> God rest ye merry, gentlemen, let nothing you dismay,
> For Jesus Christ, our Saviour, was born on Christmas day,
> To save us all from Satan's pow'r when we were gone astray.
> O tidings of comfort and joy, comfort and joy,
> O tidings of comfort and joy.

Rather than watching at a distance, in this song God becomes one of us. Born on Christmas Day, Jesus Christ, the Son of God, becomes part of the life of this floating planet, blue and beautiful ... a part of history. The carol presents Jesus as God's way of getting involved, bridging the gap between heaven and earth, becoming actively engaged in the affairs of the world: "to save us all from Satan's pow'r when we were gone astray"; to lead us beyond the forces of selfishness, arrogance, violence and alienation and to draw us to reconciliation and communion.

The picture is very different, isn't it, from that of God watching from a distance? God's watching from a distance represents a very different theological perspective from taking flesh and becoming one of us, from *incarnation*.

Looking back to the prophet Isaiah, the Christmas liturgy sees in Jesus a "child born for us," a "son given to us," as "Wonderful Counsellor, Mighty God, Everlasting Father, Prince of Peace," whose authority shall *"grow continually"* towards *"endless peace."*

Listen again to how Titus 2 expressed this same sense of movement and direction: "The grace of God has appeared, bringing salvation to all, training us to renounce impiety and worldly passions, and in the present age to live lives that are self-controlled, upright and godly, while we wait for the blessed hope and the manifestation of the glory of our great God and Saviour, Jesus Christ."

It is in becoming one with us, and drawing us into the wonderful possibilities which Christ's birth heralds, that God "rests us merry," that on this fragile blue planet, God secures us in our watching and waiting for the "blessed hope and manifestation of glory."

The incarnation is about God's involvement with the world, even identification with the world. In the person of Jesus, God becomes part of this fragile world, part of human history. In his subsequent life and ministry, Jesus demonstrates divinely human potential for bridge building, peacemaking and reconciliation. In his dying and rising, he embodies the inevitability of the final triumph of goodness. In his ongoing presence among us and within us, he invites and draws all humanity into a movement within which the final triumph of peace and goodwill is inevitable because it is the will of God. It is in this confidence that Christians "make merry" at Christmas.

I find that even the word "merry" is fascinating. Most of us use it only in connection with Christmas. It is not the quiet contentment or happiness of an individual person, but a more active, communal, even rowdy form of rejoicing. Merriment is something that we make. In the words of the carol, God not only invites merriment, but "rests us merry," keeps us merry, sustains us in merriment. God's presence keeps stirring the "merriment punch bowl." God continues to bridge the distance between heaven and earth.

The Christmas mystery pictures God, not watching from a distance, but bridging the distance between heaven and earth by taking flesh even today in those who bear the name of the only begotten Son, who share his spirit, who are members of his body.

God rest ye merry.

Merry Christmas to all.

Coming Home to Wisdom, Age and Grace

Holy Family

1 Samuel 1.11, 20-22, 24-28
Psalm 84
1 John 3.1-2, 21-24
Luke 2.41-52

Consistent with his approach in the whole of chapters 1 and 2 (the Infancy Narratives), Luke tells this story with a clear sense of purpose and direction. As a young boy, Jesus makes the journey to Jerusalem for the Passover with his parents. He gets "lost" in "his Father's house," only to be found by his parents on the third day. He returns with them, is obedient to them, and grows in divine and human favour.

I'm sure that it's the anxiety of his parents, understandable for all of you who have children—their efforts not only to find him, but *to figure him out*, their perplexity at his rather cool response when they do find him among leaders and teachers beyond their interest or experience; his mother's ongoing pensive wondering about all that is happening, and her treasuring the experience—that has contributed so much to the attractiveness of this story for parents and families.

It could be, and even probably is, our experience of gathering with family during the Christmas season—or wishing that we could, or for some reason being glad that we can't—that evokes many of these same bittersweet elements. There's life as a journey, and the ways in which we grow and change as individuals; there's the loneliness of feeling in a completely different space from someone we love; there's the joy of discovery and rediscovery, there's trying to figure out, wondering pensively and treasuring; there's homecoming and hoping, as a former translation worded the texts, for continued "wisdom, age and grace."

More than reporting historical details, Luke is "pushing these buttons." He is inviting us to meditate on these themes that will be fully developed only later in the gospel and Acts. The story is told, not so much to show how precocious Jesus was as a child, or to show his subsequent humility in being obedient to his earthly parents, as to introduce his adult faith journey.

The stories of Jesus' childhood parallel those of his adulthood. This journey to the temple parallels his journey to Jerusalem for that great final Passover, his questions about and struggle with a traditional faith culture that seems too limiting, his ultimate obedience to God in accepting the cross, and his passage through resurrection and ascension to his "Father's house." Do you see the parallels, the connections?

Listen for a moment to a section from Rainer Maria Rilke's *Letters to a Young Poet*. Does it reflect anything of the dying and rising that takes place in your own relationships with family and friends? Does it reflect what's going on in the gospel story?

> *For one human being to love another human being*: that is perhaps the most difficult task that has been entrusted to us, *the ultimate task*, the final test and proof, the work for which all other work is merely preparatory. Loving *does not at first mean merging, surrendering, and uniting with another person*—it is a high inducement for the individual to ripen…. Once the realization is accepted that even between the closest people infinite distances exist, *a marvellous living side-by-side can grow up for them*, if they succeed in *loving the expanse* between them, which gives them the possibility of always *seeing each other as a whole and before an immense sky*. [emphasis added]

Now listen to this:

> "Child, why have you treated us like this? Look, your father and I have been searching for you in great anxiety."
> "Why were you searching for me? Did you not know that I must be in my Father's house?"
> He was obedient to them … his mother treasured all these things in her heart…. Jesus increased in wisdom and in years, and in divine and human favour.

This all-so-human story—this Christmas season story—celebrates the great paradox of being family, and the dying and rising that takes place in healthy and happy homes: in holy families. The scriptures call us to be "at home" and to be "leaving home" at the same time. We are reminded that it is only in giving each other the freedom to journey that we give each other the freedom to be at home.

There is real adult experience here: the recognition of the unique relationship that persons are called to have with God; the challenge to settle only in the "Father's house"; the invitation to accompany each other along the way, sharing as best we can what this journey is all about. Jesus, Mary and Joseph have gone the road before us.

Wisdom, age and grace. Indeed.

Lament at the Absence of an Angel

Mary, Mother of God
January 1

Numbers 6.22–27
Psalm 67
Galatians 4.4–7
Luke 2.16–21

The angels had left them ... and the shepherds went with haste
and found Mary and Joseph, and the child lying in the manger.

Although she had neither seen nor heard the choir of angels
coming and going back into the heavens, Mary had a good idea of
what that experience was like. The call to "Fear not," and the sense
of wonder and privilege that followed, these she remembered, for she
too had experienced the coming and going of an angel, the angel
Gabriel ... nine months ago now.

Mary knew even better than the shepherds what it was like to get
up and get going. She hadn't just taken an evening off, but had left
everything behind and hurried to the hill country of Judea. She went
there in such haste to support her elderly relative Elizabeth, who was
also expecting a baby. Elizabeth, the wife of Zechariah the priest, lived
just outside of Jerusalem.

And now, here she was in Bethlehem, in a cave, far from family
and friends. Her promised baby was born, and she thought again about
the angel's message. The angel was gone and now the shepherds were
gone too. It was quiet; they were alone.

"And Mary treasured all these words, and pondered them in her heart."

When I was in the seminary, one of the students, a candidate for ordination in the Episcopal Church, sang a very striking song as part of evening prayer. I think it was in connection with the Feast of the Triumph of the Cross and the Feast of the Sorrowful Mother, which fall back-to-back in September.

I wish I knew where to look for the text, which had been set to music by Henry Purcell. Mary is singing, and she's shouting after the angel. The language is more elegant than this, but the song has her saying: "Gabriel, Gabriel, where are you? The nerve of you to leave me alone! Where are you when I really need you? Gabriel, Gabriel!"

The song is Mary's lament at the absence of the angel when her son was growing, yes, in wisdom, age and grace, but not in ways she had anticipated or hoped for. Home with her for thirty years ... underfoot? Then the desert, the baptism, the coming home again, only to be practically thrown over the hill. All that walking, all that talking, all those parables, and all those people: the sick, the possessed.... Then Jerusalem! She could see a horrible end coming! "Gabriel, Gabriel, where are you?"

But ... what else might she have anticipated? Isn't it true that when God wants an important thing done in this world, or wants a wrong righted, God goes about it in a very singular way? He sends a baby!

The great events of this earth are not battles, elections, earthquakes or thunderbolts, but *births*. Didn't Mary realize that? And birth is just the beginning!

Mary must have known about Sarah, poor old Sarah, raising Isaac "on the move." And that father of his! Insisting on "moving on and on," looking up at the stars, and talking to God besides!

Mary must have known about Moses' mother. She and her daughter put Moses in a basket, hoping that someone would rescue him from certain death, his fate as a Hebrew. Mustn't she have struggled with this son of hers, rescued from the bulrushes, just the first of his many risky "adventures"?

What did Mary expect? After all, she was a parent, and no reasonable parent expects a smooth and easy road.

Key to biblical faith, especially in this season when we focus on the mystery of the Incarnation, is the truth that God's spirit is not released among us by crashing thunderbolts or rollicking earthquakes, but by people being born.

New babies tell us that God has not given up on us yet. God is not yet totally discouraged with human possibilities, God is still expecting and longing for the possibilities of peace on earth, good will to the whole universe.

In a unique and wonderful way, God becomes a baby in Mary's son, and being a baby is just the start ... for him, and for her.

Mary, like all mothers, learns gradually to "treasure words like these," "pondering in her heart" the wonderful works of God, however painful they may be as she lives them from day to day.

Mothers and fathers, and friends too, need to ponder and treasure their vocation to support and nurture persons called to bring the reign of God into the future. We may even need to call out to angels from time to time with shouts and tears.

Surely Mary is unique as the Mother of Jesus, but don't we all share her vocation and her experience in our own mothering of God into the future, of mothering the eternal Word?

Stargazers and Temple Dwellers

Epiphany

Isaiah 60.1-6
Psalm 72
Ephesians 3.2-3a, 5-6
Matthew 2.1-12

"*Creator alme siderum,*" we used to sing at Vespers during the Christmas Season. "Loving, nurturing, mothering creator of the stars." *Alme Creator,* "nourishing creator," is like the *alma mater,* the "nourishing mother" that we use to describe a school we attended.

How often the sight of a star fills us with delight. It is awesome to stand outside and behold a star-studded night. I think that's one of the things I like best about going to a cottage on Lake Superior in the summer. There are no city lights to compete with the stars. The stars, it seems, have always called us to awe and wonder. They stir a sense of mystery within us. Poets write and sing about the stars. Artists paint them. In fact, the desktop on my computer features a Van Gogh masterpiece of a sky full of stars. It may even be called "Starry Night."

> Star of wonder, star of night,
> star with royal beauty bright,
> westward leading, still proceeding,
> guide us to Thy perfect light.

Of the many ways in which we might picture glory, this feast offers a guiding star, mysteriously enchanting the wise. What better way is there to picture openness to infinity than by gazing into the heavens?

The wise in the story are those who are able to welcome the new star as a gift from *Creator alme* and not as a threat. These gift-bearing stargazers come mysteriously, with courage and with wisdom, to seek one greater than themselves, then disappear without a trace. They are signs of hope, signals of the unexpected, gratuitous aspects of life's possibilities. They come from afar, and are clearly contrasted with complacent "temple dwellers" who think they already see the light.

I like to emphasize the irony of the story when I proclaim this morning's gospel. The wise men are looking for a *new king,* "for we observed his star at its rising and have come to pay him homage." King Herod is frightened, and all Jerusalem with him. He called all the chief priests and scribes of the people together for an enquiry. *All Jerusalem, all the chief priests and scribes.* This was a big deal, and they even came up with Bethlehem as his birthplace.

After what was clearly much commotion, Herod tried to calm things down by calling the wise men back for a secret meeting, but the word was already on the street. Wouldn't you think that at least some of the people would have joined up with their interesting visitors from the East? Wouldn't you think that at least one or two curious kids would have followed them to Bethlehem?

The star was shining away up there for all it was worth—and it was moving! But these temple dwellers just couldn't get it together to move out and check it out. The stargazers could.

"Darkness shall cover the earth, and thick darkness the people; but the Lord will arise upon you." The star is the loving gift of *Creator alme siderum*—a nourishing God who wants nothing more than your *alma mater* tried to give you: a sense of direction, courage, energy and curiosity to keep you growing and learning.

Even in our own thinking about social and economic matters, is there not a temptation to be, not stargazers, but temple dwellers? From time to time, do we not detect in ourselves and in the church a sad, bitter, nostalgia for a past that will never come back? Do we know people, or recognize a side of ourselves that would prefer to look down than up, backward than forward? Do we recognize something of the temple dwellers in ourselves? Epiphany invites us all to look for and reach for a new star.

Father Con Herlihy, a beloved Oblate priest and pastor in Ottawa for many years, is quoted as having written the following to his provincial superior. He was seventy-nine at the time and was offering himself for full-time ministry:

Pray not for easy lives ... Pray to be a stronger person.
Pray not for tasks equal to your powers ... Pray for powers
equal to your tasks.

He sounds like epiphany, doesn't he? A stargazer.

Star of wonder, star of night,
star with royal beauty bright,
westward leading, still proceeding,
guide us to Thy perfect light.

God's Choice

Baptism of the Lord

Isaiah 40.1–5, 9–11
Psalm 104
Titus 2.11–14; 3.4–7
Luke 3.15–16, 21–22

A voice came from heaven: "You are my Son, the Beloved; with you I am well pleased." ... Jesus was about thirty years old when he began his work. He was the son (as was thought) of Joseph, son of Heli ... son of Seth, son of Adam, son of God. (Luke 3.22, 23–38)

One of the interesting features of Luke's gospel is that the genealogy of Jesus follows immediately after the account of his baptism, which we have just heard. Beginning with Joseph, who is clearly not his "real" father in Luke, we move through a series of eleven groupings of seven generations to "son of Seth, son of Adam, son of God."

In this list of seventy-seven generations (seven being a number signifying a kind of fullness or completeness) we reach Jesus who, coming out of the waters, is the new Adam. As the Spirit breathes over the waters in Genesis, so the Spirit is breathing over the waters at Jesus' baptism, and in Luke's second volume, the Spirit will be rushing into the upper room breathing life into the first generation of the church.

Clearly something fresh and new is happening here. The world is being reborn, the human family is being offered a fresh start. As the word is creating the universe, so is the word recreating the universe. As Adam is called "son of God," so is Jesus called "son—beloved son."

After Luke's pronouncement that Jesus is "son of Adam, son of God," we find him in the desert, the reverse of paradise, where he, like Adam, is tempted.

Because Jesus resists the devil's temptation, Luke suggests, Jesus' messianic role will be to lead humanity back to the Garden of Eden. "Today you will be with me in paradise," he promises the thief from the cross. It is in a garden that Jesus will meet the devil again, on the night before he speaks those words of hope. He will be lifted up on the Tree of Life, before being buried and rising from yet another garden.

I'm placing the baptism of Jesus into this broad context to make sure that we do not miss the point which Luke is trying to make. According to Luke, God has made a choice. At the moment of his son's baptism, God announces that choice: that human history has a new beginning in the person of Jesus: in him humanity has a way to go right back to the beginning and start over. Our baptism into Jesus gives us a place in a new genealogy, taking its start from him. Less about the "salvation of individual souls," Christian baptism will be about the renewal of humanity.

What an extraordinary challenge! Baptized into his Spirit, "sons and daughters in the Son," both individual Christians and the church at large, to be true to Christ, must have this orientation, this exalted agenda.

As the year of Luke unfolds we will meet Jesus in our Sunday celebrations, where he consistently presents the consequences of this renewal: that we let go of old sins, that old divisions cease, that old debts be forgiven, that all be one in his Spirit.

Madeleine Albright, the American Secretary of State in the Clinton administration, last year addressed the graduates of the University of California, Berkeley, and described how far we are from the ideals proposed in all of these converging biblical images. She was quoted in the *New York Times* as saying:

> During the century just past, we humans learned how to transplant hearts, fly spaceships, clone sheep, and squeeze a library's worth of data into a single slender disk. But as world events reflect, we remain far from mastering the art of human relations. We have invented no technology that will guide us to the destinations that matter most.
>
> After two world wars, the Holocaust, multiple genocides, and countless conflicts, we must ask how long it will be before

we are able to rise above the national, racial and gender distinctions that divide us and embrace the common humanity that binds us.

The answer depends not on the stars or some mysterious forces of history: it depends on the choices that you and I and all of us make.

Yes, we have to make choices but, according to Luke, God has made a choice for reconciliation and communion in the person of Jesus who is declared *son* at his baptism. In our own baptism we, too, adopted daughters and sons in the *son*, are drawn into that choice.

Did you notice that Albright makes no mention of religion as a potential source for unity and reconciliation? As a descendant of Holocaust survivors, she was unlikely to refer in her speech to religion as unifying or reconciling. Does this omission invite a question such as: Is religious faith a source of human communion, or is it an obstacle? History gives all too many examples of religion and religions as barriers to human communication and communion.

Let's move on to another woman, a very different woman, the artist Judy Chicago, who expresses in her own way what Luke envisions as the goal of Jesus' life, death and resurrection, and the goal of all who are baptized into this mystery.

And then all that has divided us will merge
And then compassion will be wedded to power
And then softness will come to a world
   that is harsh and unkind
And then both women and men will be strong
And then no person will be subject to another's will
And then all will be rich and free and varied
And then the greed of some will give way to the needs of many
And then all will share equally in the Earth's abundance
And then all will care for the sick and the weak and the old
And then all will nourish the young
And then all will cherish life's creatures
And then all will live in harmony with each other
   and the Earth
And then everywhere will be called Eden once again.
   Quoted in *A Reconciliation Sourcebook* (Chicago: LTP, 1997), page 197.

They Have No Wine

Second Sunday in Ordinary Time

Isaiah 62.1-5
Psalm 96
1 Corinthians 12.4-11
John 2.1-12

People are always fascinated by the wonderful story of the transformation of water into wine, especially because of how the story is laid out in John's gospel. This story, which is not found in any of the other gospels, appears very early in John's gospel. It is Jesus' first public encounter, the first of his great signs. Some points in the story help us see precisely how it works and its depth of meaning.

Take, for example, the fact that Jesus doesn't call his mother "Mother" but "Woman." "Woman, what has this to do with me or with you?" In other words, keep your nose out of other people's business. She must have been quite a character, because then she starts bossing the servants around—which is completely out of line! In our culture, it would be the father of the bride who would do that. In the culture of Jesus' time, the bridegroom would do it, but a guest—and a woman besides—certainly would not. But Mary's role in this story is simply not at that level.

"Woman." The term is used in the first pages of the Bible, for it is the name given to Eve. Very solemnly Jesus calls his mother "Woman," just as he does when she is standing at the foot of the cross. She represents the whole of humanity; what she has to say is so sad. Speaking for the whole of humanity, Mary says, "They have no wine. There's no more joy. No more toasts are being proposed, no more glasses raised. No more treaties or agreements are being signed and celebrated. There's no more intoxication in life. No more zip, no more moment when people's defenses are lowered and they let their real

44

selves show through without the masks." Eve, announcing that they have no wine.

The lectionary omits another important detail at the beginning of the story: this encounter takes place on the third day. On the third day Jesus goes to a wedding in Cana; on the third day he rose from the dead. The story of the wedding feast at Cana points to another Triduum, another great sign of glory, another moment of exultation, of triumph, of faith. John includes these details to make us understand who Jesus is for us, who he is for all of humanity represented by Mary herself.

And there are six jars—not four or eight, but *six*, pointing therefore to the possibility of a seventh: fullness, perfection. There are seven days in the week, seven choirs of angels. Seven is the number of fullness, of wholeness. What were these six water jars used for? Ritual purification: to wash hands and feet, to make one worthy to stand in God's presence, to make one worthy to celebrate the wedding. Each held one hundred litres. Imagine. Six hundred litres of wine, all of a sudden presented to the steward who hints that some of the people are tipsy already. You usually serve the best wine first and the inferior after, when everybody is drunk, and here Jesus brings this fine wine now. The impression is that the party is well along. Six hundred litres of wine! Even if every person were to have a half a litre, that would be 1200 people at that wedding. That's an enormous project, altogether out of proportion to the reality at hand, and yet that wine will run out someday because 600 litres aren't endless. The seventh jar isn't filled yet.

Jesus says to Mary, "My hour has not yet come." Later in John's gospel, Jesus speaks about his hour at another table. And, at that table, he speaks about the vine and the branches. "I am the vine, you are the branches." Remain in me, be cleansed, be purified; discover within yourself the potential to produce wine in abundance, this year and next year and the next year and the next year—not just 600 litres but forever. Be grafted onto a source of life, a source of joy, a source of beauty, of commitment, of covenant, of agreement, of sealing and signing and intoxication and openness and simplicity. Recognize that grafted onto this vine, you have within yourself the potential to produce fruit in season and out, to tap into the seventh jar.

This story points to Jesus risen from the dead, at his hour of glory on the great third day. Layer after layer in this story helps us understand the mystery of the eucharist that we are celebrating today. Jesus appears to us, comes to us and touches us, not just in the flat, hard bread of affliction but in the joy of agreement, of community, of covenant, of toasting, of intoxication, of liberation. The great third day, the great Sunday, the hour of glory and transformation, the wine in abundance that we have in our connection with him and our connection with each other: this is the mystery of the cup that we share. Never again does anyone have to say, "We have no wine. There's no more life for us"—because Jesus has risen from the dead. His life-giving spirit, deep within us, invites us to be grafted onto his own reality, share his own glory, partake of his own abundance. The six jars of ritual purification, of unworthiness, are transformed by a seventh, his open heart—source of blood and water for the sacramental life of the church. The wine, the very substance of the person of Jesus himself, offers us hope and life, promise and joy. Drink deeply.

The Gift of Tears

Third Sunday in Ordinary Time

Nehemiah 8.1-4a, 5-6, 8-10
Psalm 19
1 Corinthians 12.12-30
Luke 1.1-4; 4.14-21

It sounds so ordinary, doesn't it? The first reading describes the liturgy of the word presided over by Nehemiah, the governor, and Ezra, the scribe, so long ago. Only a few details set it apart from the experience that we all have week after week right in this place. The men, the women and the children who can understand are gathered. Someone climbs to an elevated dais and reads from a holy book. Today's text indicates that the readings—the exposition of the wonderful truth of God's great love and mercy—took place from early morning to midday. That was a long service! The dais was outside because the temple was still in ruins. The people responded with their Amens, raised hands and tears. And Ezra said, "If you're going to cry, don't cry out of guilt or sadness, but weep because of your connectedness to what you heard. Cry tears of joy and commitment, and then go home and organize for yourself a feast."

It had been some seventy years since they could proclaim that word. Generations hadn't heard it. Imagine the emotions of the old people whose parents had told them about being deported from Jerusalem and who had suffered as slaves in Babylon and had raised their children there, trying as best they could to communicate the ancient tradition. Those people gathered once again in the holy city outside the walls of the ruined temple. And Nehemiah, who was a very devout man, and Ezra, the priest, the scribe, who is really the founder of modern Judaism, got up to read and teach. Tears, tears of joy, tears of connection, tears of commitment to a future that was unfolding for them.

My mother likes to tell the story of her visit to the former Soviet Union in 1970. With a group from her church, she visited St. Petersburg and its cathedral that had been turned into a science museum. The guide explained how it once had been called St. Petersburg, but after Lenin became the Prime Minister of the Soviet Union, the name had been changed to Petrograd to set it apart from the superstitions and the "silly old traditions of the past"—the empire, the Czarist tradition with which the church was so closely identified in their thinking. After Lenin died, Petrograd was changed to Leningrad to take it even a step further from that tradition of St. Petersburg. One of the ladies in my mother's group asked the guide if any religious services were ever held there anymore or if anybody ever prayed there. The guide responded, "We don't do that anymore. We're free of all that. We've been free of that for generations and there's no going back." My mother wondered to herself, "How does she know?"

Do you remember the coverage that was given to the re-opening of the church in Ukraine at Christmastime a few years ago? Imagine the people's experience as they gathered in a place like this, covered by a rounded dome that is much more elaborately decorated than ours. Imagine the iconostasis, and all those candles. It would be somewhere around January 6 or 7, since that's how they calculate Christmas according to the Julian calendar. Imagine them gathered there, probably for the first time since 1917, and hearing an old, old priest, who had been trying to pass on the tradition underground, read the story of the birth of Jesus—the stories of Bethlehem and the coming of the Magi. Try to imagine the tears in that congregation as they rediscovered their culture, their civilization, their spirituality, their piety, their story, their life, their symbols, their soul. "There's no going back." That guide was naive and silly. It's part of our life.

Within our own Western Christian tradition, St. Ignatius of Loyola, in the first week of his Spiritual Exercises, asks participants to do something that seems rather strange: to pray for the gift of tears. What he is really asking is that they pray for the gift of compassion, for the gift of connectedness to what they are about, for a passionate connectedness to the holy, to the sacred, to a relationship with God. Perhaps we, who take so much of this for granted, need to pray for and seek the gift of passion, the gift of a passionate connection to the wonder of God's love and mercy for us.

Religious freedom lies at the core of so many other freedoms that we take for granted in our society. We elect people. We have accountability. We have a constitution. We have a free press. We have an ability and an opportunity to participate in all these processes, to discover our own values and to incarnate them in the structures of our own society. But the number of people who actually vote or who are registered members of political parties is really rather low. We have the freedom to be involved in our church, in our parish. We have the freedom to take church envelopes, to sign up for pastoral council. We have the freedom to do all kinds of things, or not. We enjoy these options in our life and in our society. We have the freedom to determine our own way of being human. We have the freedom to determine how we wish to structure our society, our worship, our life, out of the wonderful traditions that we have inherited.

The story of Nehemiah and Ezra and their ancient people invites us to pray in the spirit of Ignatius of Loyola for the gift of tears, for a passionate commitment to the freedoms that we enjoy. It invites us to pray for a passionate commitment to a sense of the sacred, the holy, the reality of God's absolute future that's open to all of us.

The Big "Pro"

Fourth Sunday in Ordinary Time

Jeremiah 1.4-5, 17-19
Psalm 71
1 Corinthians 12.31–13.13
Luke 4.21-30

The archbishop has designated this as "Pro-life Sunday." Especially in light of the wonderful scripture texts which we have just heard, let's explore the theme together.

Take the text from Jeremiah. Jeremiah is a young adult at this stage of his career. As he presents himself before God, he recognizes something very deep and important in his mind and heart: his dignity as a human person. He recognizes that even before he was conceived in his mother's womb, God knew him. Even before he was born, he was consecrated, anointed to have a wonderful and unique place in God's plan. He looks forward to the challenges of his vocation, to the obstacles he will face, to the controversies he will stir up. Before God in prayer, he is ready for his life.

I can't help thinking about his parents, how he must have been raised, the kind of background that would have facilitated his being so full of confidence, so full of grace.

Take the text from Luke about Jesus in the synagogue. The reading continues from last week when we heard Jesus reading from the prophet Isaiah: "The spirit of the Lord is upon me ... to bring good news to the poor, liberty to captives, sight to the blind." Jesus rolls up the scroll and says: "The spirit of the Lord is *upon me*. This text is being fulfilled." He must have known that the people would say: "Who does he think he is? Isn't this Joseph's kid?" They said that all right; even more, they took him out and tried to throw him over the cliff, but he stood his ground. "Jesus passed through the midst of them and went on *his way*." Like Jeremiah before him, Jesus passed through the fear and anger of others to his own truth and integrity. He is already passing from death to life, a journey that he will complete many chapters down the road in Jerusalem. Like Jeremiah before him, Jesus too is ready for his future.

Once again, I can't help but think of his parents, Mary and Joseph. All the gospels hint that he was not an easy son to raise. What must have been his background with them which gave him, as a young man, so much confidence and grace?

When I was a student in theology, my pastoral project was to be "big brother" to Louie, a young boy who was probably about twelve years old. His mother was single and they lived in a trailer park. They were what we would call today "working poor" or perhaps even "marginal." Louie and I had a little pact. On Sunday afternoon, I would show up at their trailer and we would spend two hours looking back over his school week and making sure he was up to speed. We would have supper with his mother and then do something else, his choice. It didn't work out exactly as planned. His mother liked country music and it was on loud. She was also very busy over the weekend with laundry and other household chores, making it virtually impossible to study in that trailer. We ended up going over to the local rectory for our two hours of work before coming back for supper. I lost track of Louie over the years, but often wondered what became of him, and cannot help comparing his chances in the world with those of so many children of his age who are in the congregation this morning.

It is in the context of Jeremiah, Jesus, Louie and the children here in church that I'd like to have us consider the pro-life issue. I'm sure that "anti-abortion" is what most of us understand when we hear "pro-life." Unfortunately, the issue is too often reduced to that. *Being pro-life has to be more than being anti-anything.*

I know that many of you have been involved in Birthright, or Saint Mary's Home for pregnant teens, and would be able to testify more eloquently than I to the state of affairs of the young women involved in those programs, for whom abortion may have seemed an easy option, but who chose something else. Now what? What will become of their children? Many of these women are far more "marginal" than Louie's mom was.

It's so much easier to raise anti-abortion placards in front of parliament than it is to raise a child!

Ask any principal or teacher about kids who are really on the edge, kids who are giving trouble, who are clearly not well motivated. It's not always the case, but most often these children lack early childhood stability, and their present behaviour could almost have been predicted. Those of you who are parents know how, even under the best circumstances, and with your best efforts, there are no guarantees that child-rearing will be smooth sailing, or that you'll get the results you hope for and expect.

If we're against abortion, what are we for? If all the people having abortions today suddenly decided to bring their children into the world, if abortion stopped tomorrow, what kind of a society would we have to have to give these potentially "marginal" Louies and Louises half a chance?

> When I was a child, I spoke like a child, I thought like a child,
> I reasoned like a child; when I became an adult, I put an end
> to childish ways.... Faith, hope, and love abide, these three,
> but the greatest of these is love. (1 Corinthians 13.11, 13)

What a wonderful coincidence that the reading from Paul today is his famous "love hymn," which calls us all to maturity and depth of commitment.

To be pro-life and pro-child is an adult responsibility, calling for faithful, hopeful and loving depth of maturity, vision and generosity.

"Amen"

Fifth Sunday in Ordinary Time

Isaiah 6.1–2a, 3–8
Psalm 138
1 Corinthians 15.1–11
Luke 5.1–11

All three of today's texts deal with living persons, living situations. The prophet Isaiah experiences his own sinfulness. He knows his story. He knows who he is. He knows what kind of people he comes from. He knows what the world around him is like. But he has this blazing insight into God's holiness, God's power, God's beauty, God's desire that all be healed, reconciled and purified by the divine fire. Isaiah has to come to terms with this insight in his own life. He has to let the fire touch him and heal him so that in turn he can be a witness of what happened to him, and what's possible for others.

Then there's Paul's story: Paul, so stubborn, so proud of his Jewish ancestry, of his knowledge, his learning, his commitment, his ongoing struggle with human weakness. What a transformation has to take place in him! He senses that it is in the struggle with human weakness that he has something to offer somebody else. Only because he knows what it's like to rise and fall and rise again can he be a messenger of comfort and inspiration and encouragement to others. In his own sinfulness he finds strength, energy and power.

And we hear too the story of Simon Peter falling down in awe before the Christ. Luke has a soft spot for Simon Peter. You remember that some of the other gospels tell the story of Simon's name being changed to Peter. Jesus tells him that he is the rock on which the church will be built and immediately Peter starts arguing with Jesus about whether or not to go to Jerusalem. He doesn't really think it's necessary. It's too dangerous. It's too risky. Stay here. Stay here where it's safe. Have a safe, pleasant, comfortable community. This is where we are. Let's relax here. Then Jesus turns around and says, "Get behind me, Satan." From Simon to Peter to Satan in just a few sentences. Jesus predicts that Peter will deny him three times.

None of that material is in Luke. Luke has Jesus praying that Simon won't fail, that he will be a source of comfort and strength to the others. In chapter 2 of the second volume of Luke, the Acts of the Apostles, Simon is the first one to tell people from far and wide, from great cities and tiny villages, in ways they can all understand, that Jesus is risen. Peter goes on to Rome where, according to the tradition, he is crucified upside down because he is not worthy to imitate Christ by being crucified in the same manner as he was. In their own time persons like Isaiah, Paul and Simon Peter undergo this ongoing journey of transformation and conversion so they can be credible witnesses to others. They know themselves. They know what has happened to them; therefore, they can share with and invite others to participate in what they have experienced.

We recently spent two full meetings of our pastoral council reflecting on adult faith development: how people grow in their faith, how they deepen their commitment to Christ, how they deepen their sense of purpose, their sense of dignity, their sense of call. We pondered what can be done in a parish setting to encourage this ongoing maturing, this ongoing conversion and transformation that are at the bottom of the stories of Isaiah, Paul and Simon.

One of the suggestions was that this transformation really happens in the Sunday liturgy. It does, if we understand and appropriate it properly, and take advantage of it. The Sunday celebration is a disciplined, regular effort we make together to be in touch with God's word, to be inspired and led by it, to be nourished and strengthened by the bread and cup of the eucharist, to go back into the world, growing, strengthened, maturing.

We spent quite a bit of time reflecting on one element: the silence where each person has an opportunity to deepen that reflection. There are three principal silences in the eucharistic liturgy. The first is at the very beginning: "My brothers and sisters, we gather in the presence of God, mindful of our sinfulness, mindful of our needs, mindful of...." It's up to the pastor or whoever is presiding at the eucharist to articulate this mindfulness, and to stop so people can reflect. That's where people are invited to be in touch with who we are today, with where we're coming from. What do I need today? How do I feel today about myself, my life, my faith? Am I bored? Tired? Sick? In pain? Worried? Am I just nowhere in particular? Am I just here? In that moment of silence, we try to come to terms with and name for ourselves where we're at before we call on God's ongoing mercy, love and fidelity and proceed to the liturgy of the word. That silence gives us a chance to situate ourselves.

It was a wonderful occasion a few weeks ago. Forty-some ladies in the parish have been a part of the bridge group for many years. Over the course of that contact they have developed strong, solid friendships and ministered to each other at many different levels of life. When we gathered for the eucharist, I asked them at the beginning of Mass to be in touch with what this group means to them. What experience have they had over the years with this group of people? What reasons do they have to celebrate today? After a moment of silence, we proceeded with the eucharist. After Mass, one of the ladies commented, "I wish you had asked me to turn to the person next to me and to share a little something of that. I wish that we had had a chance to talk about that, to name our experience as a part of this group." That's an example of situating ourselves, Sunday after Sunday, of being in touch with who we are as we proceed.

The second major silence follows the homily. The readings have been read. The homily has been given. Where am I now? What am I thinking now? What did I learn? Was I comforted? Was I encouraged? Was I given a bit of a kick in the pants or was I just bored with it all? Where am I with the liturgy of the word today? What do I see myself doing with this word?

The third major silence comes after communion. It has two functions: to give us time to pray in thanksgiving for the gift of the eucharist and to catch our breath before we're sent back home. Where am I going with this nourishment that I've been given? What ongoing conversion and transformation needs to take place in me so that I can be more fully an adult Christian in the world? How am I a slightly different person because of this holy food that is inside of me? It is becoming part of me and I am becoming part of the Christ who is consuming me and whom I have consumed. What is this communion? What is it making happen in me?

The three major silences within the course of the liturgy give us an opportunity to deepen our own personal contact with God, our own personal sense of call to ongoing conversion and adult development. The first conclusion of the meeting was that rather than develop new programs, new meetings or gatherings of people, we should be clearer and more intentional about what we do when we gather here on Sunday as a community and as individuals. In that way, we can seize the opportunity the liturgy offers to grow in our faith. The second conclusion was a hope to invite people to come together in the fall to discuss the possibility of smaller groups within the community, smaller groups of friends who would meet for prayer, sharing faith and nurturing the ongoing development of our life in Christ. This would be less formal than what we do here. The third resolution was that there be in the bulletin every Sunday a couple of ponder points that arise out of the liturgy of the word. People could take these home, think about them during the week, even discuss them with their families or friends.

The point of adult faith, growth and development, then, is to be in touch with ourselves, to relate with the majesty and the mystery of God, to let God's fire purify us in an ongoing way, to let God help us to be fishers of other people in our own time and in our own space, so we can overcome our fears, our anxieties, our worries—all the obstacles that keep us from being fully alive in God. The liturgy offers direction and nourishment; it is especially in those silences that we have a chance to seize the opportunity to say "Amen" to it in the depths of our being, and really make it our own.

In Your Face

Sixth Sunday in Ordinary Time

Jeremiah 17.5-8
Psalm 1
1 Corinthians 15.12, 16-20
Luke 6.17, 20-26

If we're honest, I think we'll all admit that we prefer the beatitudes from Matthew's Sermon on the Mount to the corresponding zingers we have just heard from Luke.

Matthew's Sermon on the Mount begins in a way that evokes interesting and contrasting images. Moses came down long ago from Mount Sinai in all its desert starkness. Coming down from that mountain, he was bearing the weight of stone tablets which themselves bore the weight of the law. Matthew's mountain is so different from Sinai, so much gentler. It is a hillside overlooking the Sea of Galilee, perhaps even covered in springtime poppies. Jesus sees the crowds on this mountain and addresses them with words of blessedness designed to influence in ways that go beyond the "Thou shalts" and "Thou shalt nots" of the commandments. Pilgrims who have the privilege of visiting the Sea of Galilee and the mountain associated with Matthew's version of the sermon are sometimes even invited to picture the scene, imagining that Jesus probably used the mountainside as a natural amphitheatre where he would have been speaking from below rather than from above. This new lawgiver is speaking from below, from in their midst rather than from above or on high.

Despite certain similarities, there are sharp contrasts in Luke's presentation of this material. First, Jesus has come down from the mountain. He is on a level stretch or plain with his disciples and a great number of other people. He stops, raises his eyes to his disciples and addresses his words, not to the crowds, but to them.

57

Second, instead of Matthew's eight beatitudes, Luke offers only four, along with four contrasting woes. They are addressed directly to the disciples in the second person. Jesus is not talking *about* the poor and the rich; he is talking *to* the poor and the rich. His point can't be missed: "Blessed are you who are poor; woe to you who are rich. Blessed are you who are hungry; woe to you who are full. Blessed are you who mourn; woe to you who laugh. Blessed are you who are despised; woe to you who are respected."

Finally, there's the language itself. There's no "in spirit" to soften the content in Luke or "process words" such as hungering and thirsting after righteousness. It's black and white, cut and dried.

I don't know about you, but I really don't like to think of Jesus raising his eyes and being so "in my face"!

The prophet Jeremiah is no less unequivocal. "Cursed is the one who trusts in human beings. Blessed is the one who trusts in the Lord."

It is clear in all this that Jesus' hearers are being challenged personally and directly to think very deeply about what matters and what does not, what works and what does not, what is real treasure and what is not, what is real food and what is not, who our real friends are and who are not. Both Jesus' approach and his language throughout Luke's gospel are not for timid souls. His consistent and purposeful use of such stark contrasts and uncompromising parallels about who's in and who's out is meant to hit us between the eyes—to be "in our face." On the plain, Jesus raises his eyes to his disciples. This is what he says and how he says it. Look out!

Week after week as Luke's gospel is proclaimed this year, we will be confronted with this off-putting, in-your-face teaching. Again and again we'll be tempted to dismiss it as hyperbole, or to find ways to rework the texts so that they better suit our mentality and our circumstances. To do so would be to miss their point. Besides, we'd be cheating ourselves, selling ourselves short, ignoring our untapped potential for life beyond the ordinary.

A friend lent me Pat Barker's wonderful novel *Regeneration*, the fictionally enhanced telling of the story of Siegfried Sassoon, on which the movie of the same name was based. In 1917, this poet and decorated war hero publicly refused to continue his military service, declaring World War I a senseless slaughter. Declared mentally unsound, he was sent to Craigrock Hospital where a brilliant psychiatrist, Dr. William Rivers, set about "restoring his sanity and sending him back to the trenches." The reader has to decide what that's all about. The novel is in your face. One cannot help but sense an invitation to discover a certain "blessedness in poverty, hunger, mourning, being despised" that is concrete and real—not "merely spiritual" or "in process."

After reading the novel, I was struck again by the point that Luke's Jesus was talking about "real stuff" when he raised his eyes on the plain. For us not to allow his eyes to meet our own would be a big loss indeed. Not to allow our lives to be challenged by both gospel blessings and gospel woes would be a great loss to our real potential to name and live out core truths and human values.

Anointed Enemies

Seventh Sunday in Ordinary Time

1 Samuel 26.2, 7–9, 12–13, 22–25
Psalm 103
1 Corinthians 15.45–50
Luke 6.27–38

Luke continues Jesus' Sermon on the Plain this week with consistently radical teaching—good news that doesn't sound like good news at all.

The command to love our enemies is not just a suggestion, nor is it something reserved for extraordinary persons in extraordinary circumstances. It is simply what must be done.

In his Sermon on the Plain, Jesus has no interest in extolling common sense or in commending reciprocal neighbourliness. To repay kindness with kindness (even greater kindness than that received) or to think of virtue in terms of fairness, equity or reciprocity is to completely miss the point of his ethical teaching. "Do not sinners do the same?"

"Be as God is," Jesus insists. "Be merciful, just as your Father is merciful."

Phrases from this such as "Turn the other cheek" and "Give the shirt off your back" are so striking that they have come into common parlance, albeit as representing quite extraordinary behaviour which Jesus seems to be insisting should be ordinary in the lives of all who hear him.

But then there's that strange promise, that *there is a reward out there* for being "merciful even to the ungrateful and the wicked." There's promise of something coming back: "a good measure, pressed down, shaken together, running over, will be put into your lap; for the measure you give will be the measure you get back."

The pairing of this text with the story of David and Saul provides an interesting "for example." The story comes out of a period in David's life where his fortunes have taken a strange turn. King Saul had clearly been impressed with David's personality and outstanding abilities, but, as can often happen, when "number two" begins to outshine "number one," there's trouble. Saul's admiration turned into jealousy. David fled to the wilderness. Even there he distinguished himself by pulling together the riffraff he found there into a formidable guerilla force. It was in the wilderness that he found Saul and his men asleep in their camp. Here was his chance. It was only his religious conviction that King Saul had been anointed by God that kept him from killing him. Saul was God's anointed one. To kill Saul, even to protect his own life, would have made David incapable of "living with himself."

Rabbi Harold Kushner became famous with his bestseller *When Bad Things Happen to Good People*. In this book, focusing largely on the Book of Job, Kushner explores the mystery of undeserved suffering and God's role in it. In a later work, *How Good Do We Have to Be?*, he focuses on another set of questions. Among other issues, he deals with our human tendency to want to "make life fair" and to do so in our own way, on our own terms—"paying people back," getting "a kick out of" inflicting suffering upon those who deserve it, seeing to it ourselves that "bad things happen to bad people."

Kushner admits how difficult it is to choose not to pay others back, and how much more difficult it is to forgive from the heart even perceived offenses and slights that may never have been intended, much less those intentionally perpetrated. He suggests that in all of this there is a mysterious reward inherent in letting go, breaking the cycle of external and internal responses and counter-responses that say that life must be fair, or try to make it so out of anger or a sense of revenge.

Luke presents us with a Jesus who is working out of that framework, who is insisting that such cycles can be broken.

Is he suggesting, at an even deeper level, that every human being is a "Saul"—an anointed one? He isn't saying it in so many words, but is that the implication? Is there even a hint here that for us to think that we can create justice by lashing out at others is not only folly, but sacrilege? To do so would be laying violent hands on God's anointed, however wicked or ungrateful.

See others as God sees them, loved and called. Be merciful as God is merciful.

In Luke's gospel, we see this lived out in Jesus himself as he moves through his own life journey to the cross. There he demonstrates the truth of what he has been teaching all along:

"Father, forgive them. They know not what they do."

In the death and resurrection of Jesus, we are invited to discover how there is healing in the very act of offering healing to another, forgiveness in the very act of offering forgiveness to another, even if not received or accepted. Gifts poured into your lap!

In Jesus himself the cycle is broken, in him divine mercy and compassion take human form, in him all persons, even the "ungrateful and the wicked" are embraced as loved, called, "anointed."

Uncommon Sense

Eighth Sunday in Ordinary Time

Sirach 27.4-7
Psalm 92
1 Corinthians 15.54-58
Luke 6.39-45

Much of the Bible is not specifically about religious truth. Much of it deals with common sense, ordinary human wisdom, which may not always be so common. Today's readings are a case in point. Both Jesus' preaching in Luke's Sermon on the Plain and the first reading from Ben Sirach are in the rabbinic tradition. They use the Jewish teaching form of a string of beads: little pearls. A blind man can't lead a blind man. Why do you try to take the speck from your neighbour's eye if you have a log in your own? No good tree bears bad fruit. We need to be in touch with this ordinary wisdom to live fully human lives.

Today's text from the book of Sirach deals with a bit of human wisdom that is very important for right living. When a sieve is shaken, the refuse appears. So do a person's faults when they speak. The kiln— the oven—tests the potter's vessels. So the test of the person is in conversation. As its fruit discloses a tree's cultivation, so a person's speech discloses the cultivation of the mind. The power of speech: how important it is in right human living.

These sayings—a stitch in time saves nine, for example—probably bring to mind persons who have taught us little bits of wisdom by what they have said. These proverbs about speech make me think of my Uncle Norbert, who died last May. My mother was in the hospital at the time so it was very important for me to go to the funeral. My cousin David, his son, was to speak at the Mass, but he couldn't bring himself to do it. So he asked me to speak on his behalf from some notes he had made. One of the things he had written down about my

Uncle Norbert was: My father never met anyone he couldn't like, at least a little bit, and never said anything to anyone about the part he didn't like. Well, my Uncle Norbert must have learned that from his father, my grandfather, who said to us a million times if he said it once, "If you don't have something good to say about somebody, don't say anything at all." We've probably all heard that from a parent, a grandparent or a teacher. The power of speech can be so hurtful. It can spread false rumours and gossip. It can insult. It can cut to the heart.

The power of speech can also stir a whole world. Take the power of the speeches of Winston Churchill or Romeo LeBlanc's wonderful speech when he was installed as Governor General. Unfortunately, many people never had a chance to hear his stirring words about the life that we share in this country, and our wonderful fortune to be free. Gentle and evocative, it was a call to reconciliation, to community. The power of speech can lead us, comfort us, nourish us and challenge us.

Consider another word, a beatitude from a very wise rabbi. You won't find it in the Bible, but in some of the other ancient Hebrew material: "Blessed are those who, having nothing to say, abstain from giving us evidence of that fact." How our speech betrays what is in our mind! How our speech betrays what is in our heart! How our speech betrays what is important to us. What do you talk about with your friends? What is important enough for you to share with somebody else? What is the quality of your speech? Over and over again the Bible tries to communicate not just religious wisdom, but human wisdom, common sense that is not as common as it should be.

Lord, I Am Not Worthy

Ninth Sunday in Ordinary Time

1 Kings 8.41–43
Psalm 117
Galatians 1.1-2, 6-10
Luke 7.1-10

"Lord, I am not worthy to receive you; say but the word, and I shall be healed." Even more literally from the Latin: "Lord, I am not worthy that you should come under my roof. Say but the word and my (*anima*) innermost being shall be made healthy."

We say this prayer at every eucharist, hesitating for a moment before we join in the movement towards the table.

Those of us who celebrate the eucharist with the residents of Medex Nursing Home on Tuesday afternoons have found tears in our eyes more than once when an elderly lady raises her voice to sing during communion ... all by herself. Some of us remember the tune from our younger days. You may remember it, too.

O Lord, I am not worthy,
  that thou shouldst come to me,
but say the word of comfort,
my spirit healed shall be.

O Sacrament most holy,
O Sacrament divine,
all praise and all thanksgiving,
be every moment thine.

The eucharist is clearly not the original context of this prayer. We have just heard how it comes from a Roman centurion, a "pagan," and that it is addressed *towards* Jesus from afar. The fact, however, that it has become such a constant feature in our liturgy and in popular piety deserves our attention, especially as we read the story in its original context today and see it paired with the prayer of Solomon in the First Book of Kings.

The occasion to which the text from Kings refers is the dedication of the temple. Solomon, who had directed the building of the temple, was raising his voice in prayer in the midst of his people. "When a foreigner comes from a distant land," King Solomon prayed to the Lord, "then *hear* in heaven, your dwelling place." The prayer reflects Solomon's broad experience as well as his wide vision for the role that the temple would play in the world and in history. Some may not consider foreigners worthy of a hearing from God, but Solomon does.

Because the Phoenicians were so much better than the Israelites as designers and builders, he had invited them to Jerusalem to undertake the immense project of building the temple. In a certain way, it was their temple too. For Solomon, at least in the enthusiasm of its dedication, the temple belonged to the world.

There is a certain logic and sense of direction in his thinking. Because the temple represents and makes present the heavenly "dwelling place of God who is One," it follows that it stands as the centre of the world. Because it is the centre of the world, peoples and nations are gathered "around" it. Because God is *one,* all in the world from north, south, east and west are free and welcome to turn their eyes to this centre in a spirit of prayer and communion. Its magnificence should invite and inspire the imagination towards the unity in spirit of all people.

There is both national pride and international breadth of vision in Solomon's way of thinking and praying. There is both a sense of the truth and uniqueness of Israel's faith, and a readiness to affirm hospitality to those "outside the camp."

King Solomon rises to pray in the midst of his people. He prays with confidence that God will be open to the world and will hear the prayers of people, whatever their origin. Whether such diverse people would contemplate becoming Jews themselves is quite another matter, and is not even considered. Religious or institutional unity is not the issue. Spiritual unity is.

In the gospel story about the centurion and his slave, Jesus is experienced as another centre of life and healing. The movement to, around and out from his very person reminds us of Solomon's vision of the temple, but is even more active.

Jewish elders are sent out to Jesus from the home of a Roman commander. Jesus himself moves out towards the centurion, who in turn sends his friends back out to him with a message. Lots of comings and goings! —and the message of the centurion?

"Lord, do not trouble yourself, for I am not worthy to have you come under my roof; therefore I did not presume to come to you. But only say the word, and let my servant be healed."

Jesus responds: "I tell you, not even in Israel have I found such faith."

Do you notice that he's not saying there's no faith in Israel? He's saying: *"not even* in Israel, where there's lots of faith, have I found *such* faith—this kind of faith."

As is the case in Solomon's prayer, whether the centurion is even considering conversion to the faith of Israel, much less becoming a disciple of Jesus, is not an issue. Healing goes out from Jesus (another kind of temple) in answer to his prayer, even from afar.

Let's get back to my first observation about how the centurion's message has found its way into eucharistic liturgy and piety. Insiders and outsiders, the worthy and the unworthy, remain issues for us around participation in the eucharist. Who's welcome to join the procession to this table and under what circumstances? Are even all baptized and confirmed Catholics worthy of holy communion? Listen again to what we say just before the procession begins: "Lord, I am not worthy—but here I come anyway."

I'm sure that I'm not alone in recognizing a certain validity in traditional guidelines for the reception of the sacraments in the Catholic Church, but feeling-sensing as well that these guidelines can't possibly be "air-tight." There needs to be room for a certain breath —the breath which is the Spirit.

I can't resist sharing a couple of examples which have touched me deeply. Let's call the couple in my first example Mr. and Mrs. Conlin. Mrs. Conlin was dying of cancer, and was being cared for in their home by her husband, who had a lot of support. It was her hope that she would be able to die at home. I brought holy communion to her weekly. Mr. Conlin was not a Catholic, but met me at the door each time with a candle and knelt at her bedside while she received.

At her funeral, virtually everyone came forward for communion except Mr. Conlin, who stayed back, kneeling in the front pew. Just as I was to go back to the altar, I felt the eyes of Mrs. Conlin's sister looking at me, seeming to suggest that something was missing. She then looked over at her brother-in-law kneeling there. I went to him and asked if he would like to receive. He wept and opened his mouth.

Let's take another example. We'll call this family the Kovacs. They lived close to the church and Mrs. Kovac was a daily communicant. Her husband was a convert to Catholicism and they had raised their children in the parish. It was Christmas Eve and Mr. Kovac's mother was visiting their home for the holidays. She was an elderly lady, and quite frail. The plan was to attend Midnight Mass, but Mrs. Kovac Sr. wasn't going to come. She wasn't very impressed with Catholics and with Catholic rules, especially about communion. She couldn't "take communion," so why should she come at all?

At the last minute she changed her mind. The family sat in the third pew from the front of the church. When communion time came, she tried to step back in the pew to allow others to cross in front of her on their way from the pew into the aisle. In doing so, she lost her balance and slumped into her seat. When one of the ushers noticed what had happened, he went into the pew, lifted her up and practically carried her to the front of the church where she "took communion" and was ushered back to her place. The poor lady had little choice. She did not "take communion." Communion took her.

Getting back to the stance of Solomon, the prayer of the centurion and the way in which it has found its way into the liturgy, and to bring this longish homily to an end: I would like to suggest that as we come forward to communion today, all of us in our unworthiness, that we do so with even more consciousness and respect than may be our normal pattern.

Are Diamonds
Only for the Rich?

Tenth Sunday in Ordinary Time

1 Kings 17.8-9, 17-21a, 22-24
Psalm 30
Galatians 1.11-19
Luke 7.11-17

It's so much easier to deal with Luke's telling of parables than with his miracle stories.

In the parables, there's almost invariably a "Go, and do likewise" somewhere in the story. As challenging as it might be to discern what this "Go, and do likewise" might mean in our own particular circumstances, at least it's there. The invitation is explicit.

Not so with the miracle stories. Haven't all of us wished that someone around here had the call to "Go, and do likewise" so that, when a child was tragically killed, for example, we could do what Jesus did—stretch out our hands and raise him up?

In listening to any gospel miracle story, we need to ask: Why is this story being told? What's the point of it? Let's ask this question about the story of the raising to life of the widow's son in Naim. Is it told just to impress? Is it told to show how much power Jesus has? That he's the biggest and the best? Paired with the story of Elijah, is it told to demonstrate how Jesus is even greater than his Old Testament prototypes? That he's able to restore people to life without all the fuss that Elijah went through, calling three times to the Lord God? That he works miracles by his own power, that he is God? Or that Christianity will supplant the faith of Israel?

We've probably all heard interpretations such as this ... all of them missing the point, in my reading. They miss the point because they are out of context. Look especially today at how Luke frames this miracle story.

It begins with a statement that is key to understanding both what follows and to its interpretation: "When the Lord saw her, he had compassion on her."

The Greek verb here for "had compassion" involves being stirred from deep within, even shaken. And what do the people observe after Jesus is "shaken," and the young man is brought back to life? They do not say that "a miracle worker, healer, or magician has risen among us," but "A great prophet has risen among us!" and "God has looked favourably on his people!" Fear (awe and wonder) seized them all and they glorified God.

Shaken by compassion, the prophet is moved to speak, to speak life and healing and resurrection, by his words and by his deeds. Shaken by compassion he brings people alive. The crowds too are shaken, moved to glorify God.

Rather than isolate the prophet from others, and set him apart from them, the miracle stories draw us in to experience a living parable of divine grace.

To illustrate this more clearly, let's move from Luke's gospel to other "gospels," where we can discover living parables of divine grace.

The Hasidic masters tell the story of the rabbi who disappeared every eve of the Sabbath, "to commune with God in the forest," his congregation thought. So one Sabbath night, they deputed one of their elders to follow the rabbi and observe the holy encounter. Deeper and deeper into the woods the old rabbi went until he came to the cottage of a crippled Gentile woman. The rabbi cooked for her, carried her firewood and swept her floor. Then when the chores were finished, he returned immediately to his home before the sun would set. Now he was ready for Sabbath re-creation.

Back in the village, the people asked the elder, "Did he go up to heaven as we thought?" "Oh no," the elder answered, "he went much, much higher than that."

In awe and wonder, we hear "good news" in this miracle story; we glorify God saying: "A prophet has arisen among us."

Here's another "miracle story," a living parable from nearer to our own time and place. It is about Dorothy Day, a remarkable woman and journalist, who set up a centre for the care of the poor in New York City and published her journal *The Catholic Worker* from that centre. I read once about how a woman came in one day and donated a diamond ring. Dorothy looked around and gave it to Betty, an old woman who lived alone and came in regularly for meals. Her co-workers were sure she would have brought it to the diamond exchange and cashed it in for the centre, but she didn't. In response to their protests, Dorothy is reported to have said something like, "She has her own ideas, her own dignity. She can sell it if she wants, and pay her rent. She can take a trip to the Bahamas if she wants. She can keep it to admire. Do you suppose God created diamonds only for the rich?"

In awe and wonder, we hear "good news" in this miracle story; we glorify God saying: "A prophet has arisen among us."

I'm suggesting here that gospel miracles are not so much about the miraculous as they are about the extravagant. Responding to these living parables of divine grace, can't we be moved to a certain extravagance—a way of being prophetic in our own time? Can we hear their invitation: "Go, and be likewise."

"If"

First Sunday of Lent

Deuteronomy 26.4-10
Psalm 91
Romans 10.8-13
Luke 4.1-13

"If": it's not the shortest word in the English language, but it's almost the shortest, and it's very problematic for us in our experience of living and being tested. The only shorter word of any real substance is the word "I," and it's problematic, too. The word "if" functions in a very powerful way as the drama of Jesus' life story unfolds in Luke's gospel. "*If* you are the son of God," the devil suggests to him, "*then* shouldn't certain things follow?" "*If* you are the son of God": twice the devil challenges him with that "if."

Luke's gospel is concerned with Jesus as the son of God. In the infancy stories of its first two chapters, the angel appears to Mary and announces to her that she will conceive and bear a son by the power of the Holy Spirit. He will be named Son of God. When the infancy narrative is finished, Jesus goes to the Jordan and there meets John. He goes down into the Jordan, the same river from which Israel emerged on its final trip to the promised land, and he hears the same words that Moses heard, for God says aloud once more, just as he had spoken of the people of Israel: "You are my son, my beloved." Immediately after the statement comes the genealogy of Jesus. Then Jesus goes to the desert where the devil challenges him: "*If* you are the son of God, then shouldn't you have all the bread you need? Can't you just take this rock and make it a piece of bread? *If* you are the son of God, can't you go through life without even stubbing your toe? *If* you are the son of God, jump. *If* you worship me, you can have all you want—authority, power, glory." The devil's tricks, the devil's lies.

Israel, the son of God, wanders for forty years in the desert, tempted and tested, wondering why, *if* God is God, they are suffering like that. *If* God is God, why isn't freedom easier? *If* God is God, why doesn't the promised land just arise for us out of the horizon? *If* God is God, and God loves us, why do we have to work so hard for a living? This is Israel's temptation in the desert.

The temptation of Adam, son of God. You know that the tree in the middle of the garden of which Adam and Eve finally ate wasn't the tree of life. It was the tree of the knowledge of good and evil. And Satan, the devil, the tempter, the liar, said, "If you eat that, you'll be on a par with God." They were already created in the image and likeness of God, which means they have intelligence, they can work at knowing. They have intelligence and freedom, but not absolute knowledge; that's not for humans to have.

The devil claims, "You can have absolute knowledge. You can have absolute truth. You can know exactly what is going to happen twenty years from now. You can know exactly what you are supposed to do so that your daughter grows up to be the kind of person you want her to be. You know exactly what causes you can engage in without looking stupid twenty days from now. You can know good and evil. You can plan. You can be in charge of life. You can be God."

Well, we can't. Adam and Eve ate the fruit, but they didn't get that gift. Would we want that gift? Could we cope with it? Look back twenty years: if you knew then what you know now, would you have wanted to know exactly how your life would have unfolded? Absolute knowledge, absolute truth: could you cope with them? As humans we can't. Jesus is tested: *"If* you are the son of God, worship me. I'm in charge of all of this business," says the devil. He knows perfectly well that he is not.

We move from day to day, trusting in God, worshipping God. We live in faith, hope and love—not knowledge. This type of living has a risk factor. You don't get your bread from rocks, but by working for it. You don't jump off the temple, and let the angels hold you up so that you don't stub your toe. You take one step at a time. You make mistakes. You blunder—and God is in all that.

At the end of this wonderful story, when the devil had finished every test he could come up with, he "departed until an opportune time." When was that? It was the night before Jesus died, in the garden when he was sweating blood, being tempted again. "Let this chalice pass from me, but that's not up to me to know. Your will be done." "*If* you are the son of God, how can you be so human? *If* you are the son of God, how can you suffer so much?" A profound temptation. This temptation is a paradigm for the different temptations we experience. "*If* there is a God, why are you sick? *If* there is a God, why is the world such a mess? *If* there is a God, why isn't there more justice and peace and grace and healing in the world? *If* there is a God, why are things so tough?" We struggle with that reality. *If* there is a God, why not get your bread the easy way? Why not compromise with evil and see what you can get? Cheat a little bit and maybe, *if* there is a God, if there is a God ....

In his memoirs, *Telling Secrets,* the novelist and theologian Frederick Buechner shares a wonderful insight. He was severely tested when he was eleven years old by his father's suicide. If there is a God, why did he leave me fatherless? If there is a God, why did my father have to suffer that tremendous, horrible alienation that he must have been experiencing when he jumped off that bridge? Over years and years, he worked out the pain, the suffering, the anguish, the doubt, the temptation to cynicism, despair and emptiness under the care of doctors, psychiatrists and friends. "It's in the scars that we discover God," he concludes. I wonder if he knew that he was quoting the Book of Revelation: the glorious wounds of Jesus, the wounds in his psyche as he struggled with the tempter in the desert and left there to go back to Nazareth. The first question they asked him after he gave his first homily on the book of Isaiah was, "Isn't this Joseph's son?" The same temptation: "Who does he think he is, talking like that?" Finally, the temptation on the night before he died.

In his wounds we are healed. We are saved by Jesus because he embraces our humanity in a unique, singular, glorious way. He is one of us in everything but sin, say both the Letter to the Hebrews and Eucharistic Prayer IV. Jesus can be our guide, precisely because he too had to deal with those big "ifs" and the "I" as well. "What would it profit someone to gain the whole world and lose themselves in the process?" he asks in Luke's gospel. He dies believing that. How could he compromise with evil? With what he understood to be right? How could he play something more than he really is? The Word-made-flesh, our Saviour, our redeemer, heals us by his glorious wounds. His story stands forever, constantly inviting all of us to deal with the temptations of life in that same spirit. He asks us not to try to protect ourselves from life's bruises, but to live fully and abundantly in faith, hope and love. He invites all of us to jump in, to participate in his own struggle with the tempter, a struggle with sin and death, with bread, with glory, with power—all the things that tempt us to be absolutely secure in our own being.

Look at the vulnerable Jesus, famished in the desert, talking with the devil about life and death. The big *if*: the agony, the cross, the glorious wounds. The wonderful stories of original sin and Jesus' temptation in the desert are inviting us to be a part of this experience of faith. Seize the depth of the stories, recognize that we participate, even now, in living those stories confidently and lovingly in our own world, with hope in the God who raised Jesus from the dead and who raises us with him.

Finding Ourselves
as Cross-Bearers

Second Sunday of Lent

Genesis 15.5–12, 17–18
Psalm 27
Philippians 3.17–4.1
Luke 9.28b–36

They were terrified as they entered the cloud.
Then from the cloud came a voice that said,
"This is my Son, my Chosen; listen to him."

According to Luke, only eight days before they climbed that mountain, Jesus was at prayer with his disciples in another place. He had asked them about the crowds, what they thought of him. They had answered with what they had been hearing, until he pushed further. "Who do *you* say that I am?" Peter answered, "The Messiah of God."

We can only imagine the looks on their faces when Jesus issued an order that they tell no one and then launched into descriptions of his upcoming rejection, suffering, death and resurrection, insisting that for *real life*, this would be their destiny as well. They must have been mystified.

Now Jesus has taken three of them to the mountain, once again to pray. The subject of his ultimate destiny comes up again. This time it's in a conversation he is having with Moses and Elijah, who mysteriously appear there with him. Transfigured in glory, Jesus is speaking with them about his "departure" which will take place in Jerusalem.

Moses and Elijah seem to be in a position to give him some advice. Their own story demonstrates clearly enough that they would know

76

what they're talking about when it comes to dealing with stressful decisions, hard journeys, misunderstanding and rejection. "Weighed down with sleep," the disciples give no indication that they heard anything of the conversation. They did see the conversation happening, however, and Peter spoke up about a shrine-building project. Jesus didn't answer, but God, overshadowing them in a cloud, said: "This is my Son, my Chosen. Listen to him."

Do you notice the progression in both scenes?

In the first scene there's prayer, conversation-questioning with Jesus and his disciples, Peter's statement, and finally the word of Jesus.

In the second scene there's prayer, conversation between Jesus, Moses and Elijah, Peter's statement, the word of God from the cloud. (The cloud of God's presence reminds us of the cloud that led Israel through the desert by day. It is from that cloud that God invites the disciples to "Listen" to his Son, his Chosen.)

In both cases the "outbursts" of Peter, who has been sharing prayer time with Jesus, seem off the mark, or at least incomplete.

In both cases, Peter's responses do not go deeply enough into the mystery of the person and mission of Jesus into which Peter and the other disciples are being invited.

The first outburst: "You are the Messiah of God." Even in our own culture, we need to learn that there's much more to an authentic Christian life than saying "Jesus is Lord," or having religious bumper stickers on our cars.

The second: "Let us make dwellings." Even in our own culture, faith can too easily be reduced to "shrine-building": great care in building clear systems of orthodoxy, or clear structures for piety.

Neither the simple proclamation of Jesus' lordship, nor the building of programs and structures for right doctrine and piety, as important as these projects might be, reflects the kind of world into which Jesus is drawing his disciples. The voice of God from the cloud seems to be insisting that the disciples pay very good attention to what Jesus has just eight days previously proclaimed to them:

If any want to be my followers, let them deny themselves, take up their cross daily and follow me. For those who want to save their life will lose it, and those who lose their life for my sake will find it. What does it profit them if they gain the whole world but lose or forfeit themselves?

Isn't the language paradoxical? It's not ultimately about sacrificing yourself, or losing yourself, but finding yourself. *The goal of it all is to find yourself.*

We used to hear more talk than we do today in popular culture about a certain kind of self-fulfillment or self-affirmation. We used to hear a lot of slogans, such as "You have to live a little," or "Spoil yourself," because "You'll be dead a long time." They were about letting yourself go, tasting each and every experience to show yourself and others that you are fully free and fully alive. Although not all bad, and a reaction to excesses in the direction of mindless (and boring) conformity, many people have learned from their own experience or that of their families and friends (even apart from religious considerations) that, when taken to excess, such an approach to life is healthy for neither body nor spirit.

To discover true freedom or to find yourself in Jesus' teaching is a much deeper matter. The question is whether you really care about yourself. Do you care enough about yourself to do right by others? Do you tap your full potential, or sell yourself short? Do you assume responsibility for yourself, or do you let yourself go? The way in which you respond to such real-life choices reflects better than anything else your quality of character. The cross is about character.

After the transfiguration, Jesus "sets his face" for Jerusalem. In inviting his disciples to follow him, he is suggesting that choosing a particular way of life or path to salvation is an essential aspect of every person's life. An individual doesn't come to life simply by thinking about it, or even praying about it, but by hitting the road. Our own identity, the stuff with which we are made, will be tested along that road by the quality of the value decisions that we make as we move along. The cross is about values.

Along the road to Jerusalem, to his "departure," Jesus himself had to make hard choices between personal integrity and public acceptance, between going through ritual motions and true faith, between being silent and speaking out, between power and service. Many of the choices we make fall into these same categories. The cross is about such choices.

Listen to how Nelson Mandela describes the same kind of experience:

> I have walked that long road to freedom. I have tried not to falter; I have made missteps along the way. But I have discovered the secret that after climbing a great hill, one only finds that there are many more hills to climb. I have taken a moment here to rest, to steal a view of the glorious vista that surrounds me, to look back on the distance I have come. But I can rest only a moment, for with freedom comes responsibilities, and I dare not linger; for my long walk is not ended.
>
> Nelson Mandela, *Long Walk to Freedom,*
> (New York: Little, Brown, 1994), page 544.

As we prepared to hear the gospel on this Second Sunday of Lent, we marked our heads, our lips and our hearts with the cross. The content of this gospel reminds us of what we are saying in that action which seals us as cross-bearers.

What's in a Name?

Third Sunday of Lent

Exodus 3.1–8a, 13–15
Psalm 103
1 Corinthians 10.1–6, 10–12
Luke 13.1–9

"Thou shalt not take the name of the Lord, thy God, in vain."
That's the way I learned the second commandment as a child, and for
years I thought it was all about "swearing." I think it was Sister Richard
in Grade 3 who taught us that it's fine to say "Jesus Christ" if it's in a
prayer (and we should also bow our heads as we say the holy name)
but it's not okay to say "Jesus Christ" if you fall off your bike and bang
your elbow, unless of course you are saying a prayer at the time, which
would not be likely. She didn't go into many other examples of swear
words, but she was sure we'd recognize "rude and coarse" language
when we heard it and would not use "those words" ourselves. I learned
later when I moved to Canada that people who spoke French had
particularly colourful ways of mixing and matching holy words.

Of course it's impolite, inappropriate, offensive to use such language, however mindlessly, but the deeper meaning and power of that
ancient commandment is reflected much more fully in the biblical
scenes presented on this Lenten Sunday.

Insurance companies call storms and earthquakes "acts of God";
trials and even executions have been carried out to protect the truth
of "God's revelation" from being corrupted; wars have been fought
"in the name of God"; accidents, sickness and death have been discussed as the "will of God." There are even certain precedents for this
kind of "God talk" in the scriptures themselves, but surely not in
today's readings.

Jesus solidly and profoundly challenges anyone who would even think of using God's name in such ways. "Do you think for one minute," he says, "that those Galileans whose blood was mingled with their sacrifices were being punished by God?—or those people who were killed when the tower collapsed?" He goes on to insist that, rather than trying to evaluate the experiences of others or relate God's will to the many uncertainties of life, his hearers should focus on conversion and growth in the spirit. The other alternative is death.

The road to life is not found in knowing God's righteousness intellectually, but in knowing God's righteousness at work in your own possibilities for righteous living. Jesus goes on to tell one of his famous tree parables, noting how patient the farmer is in waiting for it to be fruitful, and giving it all it needs in the meantime—but even that wonderful care cannot substitute for the tree's own inner resources, and time is not to be wasted. It's not about "God talk," but about active partnership with God's living presence.

Awesome! Is that word still current among young people? I don't think I've heard it as much lately as I used to. The story from Exodus about the call of Moses from the burning bush is truly awesome. I'm sure I'm not alone in my opinion that it's one of the most important texts of the whole Bible. The scene is Mount Horeb, later called Sinai. It's no coincidence that on Horeb, God tells Moses his name and on Sinai (the same mountain) God warns that THE NAME is not to be taken in vain. Israel took that commandment so seriously and held God in such deep respect that THE NAME was pronounced only once a year by the priest in the temple's holy of holies. Since the destruction of the temple, it is not spoken at all. For a while, we Christians used THE NAME in our public reading of the scriptures and in some of our hymns. More recently, out of respect, we too refrain from speaking or singing THE NAME in our liturgies.

When I was on sabbatical, I had the opportunity to visit Mount Sinai. We climbed it to watch the sun rise on what, for the Greek Orthodox, was Easter Monday, and later visited Saint Catherine's Monastery. There's a very unusual bush in the monastic compound that the monks believe to be a descendant of the bush found in today's story. It's an amazing place—awesome—and I wish we could all go there right now to live the context of this story.

Today we'll have to be satisfied just with the story. While Moses is looking after his sheep, he sees a fire in the distance that just isn't going out. It's a burning bush—an eternal flame—a traditional symbol of divine presence. Moses hears a voice calling his name, obeys the voice, and removes his shoes as he is told to do. To remove your shoes is a traditional sign of respect still observed among Muslims.

When God begins to speak again, Moses covers his eyes because the fire is so bright that he is afraid of being blinded. The sense later grew in Israel that no one could see the face of God and live. God reassures Moses by identifying himself with the God of his ancestors, with the presence of constant love and protection, with the possibility of freedom from slavery, and with a bountiful land where they could establish their own homes. Moses asks what so many of us would still ask: "What is your name?"

If we know somebody's name we can track them down, we have at least half a chance of finding out where they live and what they're all about. Moses feels he has to know God's name in order to talk to the people about this strange and marvellous encounter. If they know THE NAME, a real relationship will be possible.

Jo and Jim, a wonderful couple from our parish, invited me to their home for dinner one evening. They had also invited their daughter Mary Ann and her children Colin and Meghan. During the course of the evening I overheard Colin talking to his grandfather and kept hearing "X." Finally, I asked what this "X" business was all about. Jim told me that when Colin was just a toddler, he asked what he should call him. Jo called him Jim, his mother called him Dad, and it was all a bit confusing for Colin. Jim responded that it really didn't matter a whole lot. "You can call me 'X', if you want." Colin has been calling him "X" ever since, and it's clearly a name of great respect and affection. "X" or whatever, names are essential ingredients in our relationships with others.

The divine name, which God offers, written in Hebrew without any vowels is, in our alphabet, the very mysterious YHWH. We are not even sure how it would be pronounced, but it is generally thought to be derived from the verb "to be." Perhaps it means "I am," or "I am who I am," or "I will be who I will be." In other words, what a name it is! "Don't fence me in," it seems to imply. "Don't put me in a box."

"Don't try to understand me or control me." "Live with me; move with me; journey with me." At any rate, it is clear that God is a verb, not a noun. God is dynamic, not static. God is a "going concern." Implied in the name is the sense that we humans, however tempting it might be, can never glibly assume that God is here and not there, behind this and not that, responsible for this and not that, rewarding and punishing this way and not that. God is somehow too big, too free ... too mysterious.

In our own Canadian context, Anglican Bishop Michael Ingram has written a book called *Mansions of the Spirit*. His book invites Christians to consider the many ways beyond "our household" where God is living and active, to reconsider our traditional understanding of and relationship with Judaism, Islam, Buddhism and the other great faith traditions of the world. He visited Ottawa where he gave a lecture at St. John's Anglican Church, which dealt with these same themes. I attended that lecture and guess I shouldn't have been surprised that the audience's response was not totally positive. It's one thing to believe that God is everywhere; it's another to risk acting on that belief.

Although he did not refer directly to this text, he invited us Christians to be stretched in the "awesome" spirit of the God of the burning bush. "*I am who I am.*" He challenged the ways in which Christianity has made and continues to make exclusive claims to the truth. Was he suggesting that we Christians have been taking THE NAME of God in vain? Many in his audience were clearly uncomfortable.

As Bishop Ingram was inviting us to broaden our understanding of the presence and action of God beyond our religious boundaries, was he suggesting that we have not been sufficiently respectful of the very name of God, of the mystery, the holiness inherent in the divine I AM? His reminding us of our ongoing temptation to Christian imperialism, and of the inherent sinfulness of such a stance over and against the world, underlines the fact that God's own sharing of the divine name, "I am who I am," is, for the Bible, a divinely revealed call to a certain asceticism that may be particularly appropriate for Lent. We are invited to give up quick and easy presumptions about many things, and to deepen our communication and collaboration with the God of the burning bush. This is the same God whose kingdom Jesus both proclaims and acclaims.

When God Believes in Us

Fourth Sunday of Lent

Joshua 5.9a, 10–12
Psalm 34
2 Corinthians 5.17–21
Luke 15.1–3, 11–32

But when he came to himself, he said, "How many of my father's hired hands have bread enough, and to spare, but here I am dying of hunger! I will get up and go to my father, and I will say to him, 'Father, I have sinned against heaven and before you; I am no longer worthy to be called your son; treat me like one of your hired hands.'"

Does this young man sound contrite, or just desperate? Does he care about his father, or just about himself? Is he sorry for his sins, or just hungry?

I was talking once with a professional counsellor who was working with a young man whom I had known since he was a kid. His life had been very troubled and nobody could steer him on track. His parents had both died tragically when he was only three or four; he had been in various foster homes and group home settings which hadn't worked out very well. His teachers, social workers and others who cared for him tried hard to get him the help "he needed," but to no avail.

The counsellor told me something I guess I had always known. He told me that most people enter therapy only when they believe they have to, after life becomes unbearable, when change is no longer an option.

The counsellor was confident that this boy, now a young man, was on the right track. He was beginning to identify and name his pain and to face it. What he would need now was the courage first of all to look beyond the pain, to imagine a better way of life, and to articulate realistic expectations. Finally he needed courage, the faith in himself to reach out and achieve new goals. As for the rest of us, "Just believe in him," the counsellor said, "and let him know that you believe in him."

In Jesus' parable, the prodigal son hit bottom and, to his credit, had the courage and imagination to begin developing at least a survival strategy. The gospel says: "He came to himself." He faced reality. As the counsellor described the three steps, he was at number one. He was naming his pain. His father asked no questions, he just believed.

We have no idea how subsequent conversations between this young man and his father developed that first night back home or in the days and weeks ahead. The story doesn't tell us. It tells us only that the father loved and believed, however contrived and self-serving his son's homecoming might seem to us. He is ready simply to proceed with an open-ended trust. What a risk!

It is the father's embrace of love and trust that stands to give his son the courage he will need to move beyond simple survival. The father's embrace of love provides not only an invitation, but also the foundation for the rebuilding of a broken and humiliated person, and the rebuilding of family and community. The father believes in his son, so anything is possible.

The father believes in the elder son as well, even in his smugness and jealousy. The father comes out to him as well. The father believes in this son's potential to recognize and appreciate his own privileged position in the house and to move on in a spirit of generosity and reconciliation. One can only imagine the pleading tone in his voice: "Son, you are always with me, and all that is mine is yours. But we had to celebrate and rejoice, because this brother of yours was dead and has come to life, he was lost and has been found."

We don't know either how conversations between this son and his father developed in the weeks and months ahead. The story doesn't go that far, but an invitation has been extended, an invitation to real life.

The parable doesn't tell us how either of the sons responded, it only tells us that their father believed in them, that he "went out to them," that he invited them to stand up and be new. We're not sure

85

about the sons, but the father, a clear image of God, has faith, hope and love in abundance.

In the 1960s, Michel Quoist, a French priest and pastor, wrote a book entitled simply *Prayers*. Imaginative and picturesque, they reflect his hopes and dreams for his own people and his own city. I see the faith, hope and love of the Father reflected in this one, called "The Swing."

> He was gently swinging at the end of the ropes.
> Eyes shut, relaxed and drifting, he listened to the
> Murmur of the breeze that sang a lullaby as it
> Swayed him back and forth.
> And minutes floated away to the cadence of the swing.
>
> So, Lord, I walk through the city as through a vast county fair,
> and see people drifting, blown by the breezes of life.
>
> Some smile, and yield to passing pleasures,
> Others with taut faces curse the wind that shakes them
> And knocks them into one another,
>
> Lord, I want them to stand up on their swings,
> I want them to grasp the cords that you hold out to them,
> I want them to harden their muscles and brace their
> vigorous bodies, and stamp on their lives the
> direction they have chosen.
>
> For you do not want your children to drift,
> But to live.

The positioning of this parable in mid-Lent (*Laetare* or Rejoice Sunday) is a wonderful invitation of love and faith addressed to us. Can we see ourselves as either or both of the sons called beyond their state of affairs to freedom, dignity and grace? Can we hear the invitation to stand up in our swings, grab hold, breathe deeply, feel our possibilities, and rejoice?

God of the Not Yets

Fifth Sunday of Lent

Isaiah 43.16-21
Psalm 126
Philippians 3.8-14
John 8.1-11

> Do not remember the former things, or consider the things of old. I am about to do a new thing; now it springs forth, do you not perceive it?

The context is the sixth century before Christ. The people of Israel are free to return home after about three generations in exile as slaves to the powers of Babylon. Their movement across the Syrian desert cannot help but be compared with that long ago Exodus from slavery in Egypt to the land of promise. Now they were going back to that land of promise, to the huge project of rebuilding.

The prophet encourages joyful anticipation of the future as the people come home. He encourages that because there are always other possibilities. People have been known to look at a great and challenging project and quit before they even begin. People are also prone to look backwards, allowing past failures to discourage new beginnings. Learn and move forward in the spirit of God.

> Jesus straightened up and said to her, "Woman, where are they? Has no one condemned you?" She said, "No one, sir." And Jesus said, "Neither do I condemn you. Go your way, and from now on do not sin again."

The woman in the gospel story is getting the same prophetic message from Jesus. Focus not on what has been, but on what can be.

Jesus, from being bent over, writing in the dust, straightens up. He stands tall and invites her to stand tall with him.

In her book *Kitchen Table Wisdom* (New York: Riverhead Books, 1996), Rachel Naomi Remen tells a wonderful story of her own "waking up" to the future.

When she was thirteen, her father declared bankruptcy. Christmas was coming, and because of their financial situation, her mother suggested that they would make their Christmas presents this year. She tried to make the whole experience positive and fun, and it was. Rachel Naomi awaited Christmas with even more than the usual anticipation, wondering if the muffler she had secretly knitted for Dad would please him, and how the bracelet she had designed with copper wire would look on her mom.

Christmas morning arrived, and the living room looked as it always had, the familiar decorations were out, and the coffee table was heaped with presents, only this year they were wrapped with the newspaper's "green sheet" which they had carefully saved over the last few weeks and tied up with last year's ribbon. Among the parcels was a small velvet box.

She looked at it with suspicion, sure that there was nothing homemade in there. "It's for you," her father said. "Open it."

She describes her reaction:

Inside was a pair of twenty-four-karat gold earrings. They were exquisite. I stared at them in silence, bewildered, feeling the weight of my homeliness, my shyness, my hopeless differ- ence from my classmates who easily joked and flirted and laughed. "Aren't you going to try them on?" prompted my father, so I took them into the bathroom, closed the door, and put them on my ears. Cautiously, I looked into the mirror. My sallow, pimply face and lank hair, oily before it even dried from a shower, looked much as always. The earrings looked absurd.

Tearing them from my ears, I rushed back into the living room and flung them on the floor. "How could you do this?" I shrieked at my father. "Why are you making fun of me? Take them back. They look stupid. I'm too ugly to wear them."...Then I burst into tears. My father said nothing until I had cried myself out. Then he passed me his clean folded handkerchief. "I know they don't look right now," he said quietly. "They were your grandmother's and someday they will suit you perfectly."

Her father believed in the person she was becoming. He believed that she would grow into those earrings. He saw something in her that she could not see in herself, or perhaps that she could *not yet* see in herself.

It's perhaps a cliché to say that a human person is not a noun, but a verb, or that each of us is a work in progress.

Jesus looks up at the woman in the gospel, and believes in her. No lectures. She knows her past well enough. He sees something more in her than her past; he sees a future. "Do not sin anymore," he says to her. Do not look for life in the wrong places anymore; begin again; believe that your life can be new.

Society and culture also are verbs: works in progress. Isn't it perhaps even harder at this level of life to believe that we can grow into the earrings? Isn't it true that there are a lot of fed-up people around who have become rather cynical about the social and political, even the religious and ecclesiastical affairs of our own time?

In his own time Isaiah believed that Israel could grow into the future, all evidence to the contrary notwithstanding. In his vision and approach, the mistakes and sins of the past become resources for the future if the community is prepared to take history's lessons to heart. Isaiah invites the community to believe in its capacity to become builders of justice and peace and invites them to stand tall and push to the future.

While I was waiting to get my hair cut a couple of weeks ago, the man in the barber's chair was moaning and groaning about the government. "They're all alike," he grumbled. "I'm so fed up, I'm not even going to vote next time" ... but he did like the idea of tax cuts. I felt like giving him a good shake. Isaiah was weeping.

The big word in faith and hope is "yet." John has not developed much self-confidence—yet. Mary is going to need a lot of courage to face that surgery. She'll find it. She hasn't found it yet, but she will.

We haven't developed a fully just and equitable society, not yet, but we're working on it.

It is in the "not yets" that we discover the presence and power of the Spirit. God is in the "not yets." We'll grow into those earrings yet.

Sustaining the Weary

Passion (Palm) Sunday

Isaiah 50.4–7
Psalm 22
Philippians 2.6–11
Luke 22.14–23.56

From the prophet Isaiah, we heard the servant of the Lord say: "The Lord God has given me the tongue of a teacher, that I may know how to sustain the weary with a word." For us Christians, this very servant came alive for us in Luke's telling of the passion.

There is such amazing grace in the tongue of this Jesus who teaches so eloquently in his dying, who knows how to sustain the weary with a word.

"Father, forgive them," he says just after he is crucified, "for they do not know what they are doing."

"Jesus, remember me, when you come into your kingdom," pleads one of the criminals crucified with him. Jesus responds characteristically, "Truly I tell you, today you will be with me in paradise." As he does so often throughout the gospel, he proclaims that there is a table set for sinners and for the poor, that the eternal feast of paradise, fruits of the tree of life from which Jesus is now hanging, are for him, too.

"Father, into your hands I commend my spirit," Jesus cries before breathing his last, teaching us how to live and die in hope. He has gone before us—"one with us in all but sin."

Listen to the teacher today, and let his forgiving, inclusive and hopeful spirit grow in you as Easter draws near. "Let that same mind be in you that was in Christ Jesus."

Note: This homily, necessarily brief, will depend for its effectiveness on how the proclamation of the passion and the homily are choreographed. I would suggest the use of the Taizé chant "Jesus, remember me ..." as the acclamation between the sections of the passion, a silence (kneeling) when Jesus "breathed his last," another silence after the passion before the presider rises and gives the homily from the place of the chair. If the whole of the liturgy of the word is proclaimed engagingly, such a brief homily, almost a reprise of the liturgy, can provide an effective bridge to the eucharist.

The Easter Triduum

Mass of the Lord's Supper

Holy Thursday

Exodus 12.1-8, 11-14
Psalm 116
1 Corinthians 11.23-26
John 13.1-15

This day shall be a day of remembrance for you. You shall celebrate it as a festival to the Lord; throughout your generations you shall observe it as a perpetual ordinance.

You *shall* remember, and you *shall* celebrate the festival—in word and sacrament, in story and ritual. A solemn commandment from the Almighty.

In this place, on this night, we begin the "Great Christian Pasch"—the great festival of three nights and three days in honour of our God. We undertake active ritual remembering, which is central to biblical religion.

Listening to stories, we undertake to make them our own in this Great Christian Pasch. We wash each other's feet; we take an offering for the poor and pile packages and cans around our table; we reach out to each other in peace; we break a common loaf; we share a common cup.

We do these things not because we are particularly good at it, or because we are *comfortable* with them, but because of the stories we have heard and the invitations offered in these stories.

"Do this in remembrance of me." "Do this, as often as you drink it in remembrance of me." "If I, your Lord and teacher, have washed your feet, you also ought to wash one another's feet. For I have set you an example, that you also should do as I have done for you."

Why is the commandment to do these things so strongly worded and so essential to the life of the church? The eminent Dutch theologian Edward Schillebeeckx suggests the following:

[Coming together in liturgical celebration] reminds us that believers deal with reality in two different ways which influence each other. On the one hand there is everyday reality, "worldly reality." On the other hand we can experience the same reality sacramentally and elevate it to a symbolic but nevertheless real level of reality.

There is everyday worldly reality in which people are often like wolves preying on each other, grabbing, and scavenging: a world of injustice and oppression, in short, a history of disaster and suffering. Many good things also happen in this worldly world, but we will never be certain whether good or evil will have the last word in it. To give form to the certainty of faith that good, and not evil, will have the last word, we need the sacramental world. This is ... liturgy.

For the Sake of the Gospel
(New York: Crossroad, 1990), page 76.

See what he's saying?

I think he's saying that in our everyday world, peoples and nations may well be moving ahead to greater autonomy and prosperity, but are the poor and oppressed among them? Are the slaves being freed?

In what Schillebeeckx calls "worldly reality," feet are being washed, to be sure, but whose feet? And for what reasons? In the everyday world, good wishes are shared, bread is broken, toasts are proposed, and wine is shared, but by whom and with whom?

In the liturgy, in story and ritual, we do all of that and get it right!

What we do *in* church is done as a signal of what we are called to be *as* church in the world. What we do here in our rituals signals what must happen everywhere else in the lives of persons who are in tune with God.

Ritual activity opens avenues for us to consider and evaluate our *worldly* activity more carefully, and to work at bridging the gap between the two. Believers engage in bridge-building activity between ancient story and contemporary reality, between liturgy and life, between being *in* church and *being* church. This process is itself a kind of "passing over." The liturgy challenges us to make what goes on *out there* more in tune with what goes on *in here*—footwashing, reaching out, breaking bread, toasting life and freedom open to all.

William Temple was the Archbishop of Canterbury during the bombing of London in the Second World War. After communion one Sunday, he is reported to have offered a second homily in which he compared his own wartime role with that of presidents, prime ministers, and generals who were trying to manage and win the battle.

He too was leading: leading the liturgy. He too was presiding: presiding over holy communion.

He saw himself inviting the assembly and the nation to look beyond "winners and losers," especially in the eucharist. The eucharist is Christ's pledge of a holy communion in which all divisions are healed, and the spirit of the whole world is one. He noted that, according to the tradition of his church at the time, kings and commoners alike knelt to take this pledge of Christ's ongoing active presence in making communion.

A famous African-American spiritual hints at this same consciousness in another worshipping assembly: "Let us break bread together on our knees. Let us break bread together on our knees. When I fall on my knees with my face to the rising sun, O Lord, have mercy on me."

The spiritual understands that in these ritual gestures, the worshipping assembly is ultimately expressing openness to the mercy of God, source of all grace and healing, which will transform the world beyond ritual.

In our own liturgy, we follow the more ancient tradition of standing, actually processing towards holy communion. In doing so, we express these same possibilities in a way that may even be more dynamic and dramatic than kneeling.

On this first night of the Great Pasch, we enter into the mystery of footwashing, bread breaking, cup sharing—symbol making—with the full confidence that God does not command in them what we are incapable of doing beyond these walls.

We enter into these ancient rituals with grace and with courage.

Celebration
of the Lord's Passion

Good Friday

Isaiah 52.13–53.12
Psalm 31
Hebrews 4.14-16; 5.7-9
John 18.1–19.42

Moving through the Great Christian Pasch, we arrive at Good Friday. We listen to the story of Christ's passion and death, and respond in ritual veneration of the cross.

As we move to and around the cross, we will be singing:

Faithful cross above all others,
One and only noble tree,
None in foliage, none in blossom,
None in fruit your peer may be,
Sweet the wood and sweet the iron,
And your burden, sweet is he.

I remember being very struck as I read a report about another ritual carried out by residents of a small village, which I believe was in Africa. Years ago, we would have called these people and their practices pagan, but today many of us are less sure of such categories.

A woman was raped one Sunday morning at the edge of her village. The following Sunday the whole town gathered at the spot. Forming a circle they walked in silence around and around the place where she had been accosted, following two women playing a heart-beat rhythm on their drums. The movement stopped. A stone was passed to each person in the group and they were asked, if they wished, to speak their feelings or prayers and to breathe them into the stone.

Animated by their collective spirit, the stone was buried. There was healing, purification and commitment to freedom and human dignity in the air and in the earth.

Is this not the sort of thing that happens at the great sites of Christian pilgrimage? Remembering a Friday long ago, are we not doing something like this right here today?

Yes, we are doing something like this, but the story that we are remembering is so different that what we will be doing will be correspondingly different.

"My kingdom is not of this world," we read in John. "I have come into the world to testify to the truth, and everyone who belongs to the truth listens to my voice. For this I was born ... I am thirsty ... It is finished." Head bowed, he gave up his spirit.

Jesus was not being raped or murdered. He was giving his life for the life of the world, and, risen from the dead, continues to breathe his spirit upon the world even today.

Faithful cross above all others,
One and only noble tree,
None in foliage, none in blossom,
None in fruit your peer may be.

In just a few moments, we will carry a cross into this place of assembly. In Jerusalem and at the Vatican, the cross carried on Good Friday was a piece of what is believed to be the true cross of Christ itself, mounted and framed in bejeweled reliquaries. Clearly it is a sign, not of death's inevitability, but of life's promise in Christ's sacrifice, in his gift of himself. As the cross is being brought in, it will stop three times. I will extend my arms towards it and chant: "This is the wood of the cross, on which hung the Saviour of the world." "Come, let us worship," you will reply.

One by one we will approach it. Some of us will bow; some will kneel; some reach out to touch it, others bend to kiss the cross. Yes, we will breathe our own faith into it, but, perhaps more importantly, it will breathe faith into us.

I wish that all of you could share the experience that I and several assisting ministers will have in balancing that big cross, trying to adjust it so that each one of you can touch it and be touched by it in your own way, and to feel and sense your varied responses. When the procession is finished, we will plant that cross right here in front of the table where it will preside over our sharing of communion ... no cup today, just the broken bread.

As the Great Pasch moves forward, isn't it evident that we are being invited to embrace the cross here and in every place where "we live, and move, and have our being"? Are we not, in the ritual gestures of Good Friday, being called to say "Amen" to the brokenness of him who makes us whole and in whom all of creation is called to communion?

In this place, we carry the cross with dignity and devotion as a sign that we are ready to carry it *beyond* this place with the same dignity and devotion.

As the Great Pasch proceeds, we enter into these rituals with grace and courage. "Lift high the cross."

Easter Vigil

Holy Saturday

Genesis 1.1–2.2
Psalm 104 or Psalm 33
Genesis 22.1-18
Psalm 16
Exodus 14.15-31; 15.20, 1
Exodus 15
Isaiah 54.5-14
Psalm 30
Isaiah 55.1-11
Isaiah 12
Baruch 3.9-15, 32–4.4
Psalm 19
Ezekiel 36.16-17a, 18-28
Psalm 42 or Psalm 51
Romans 6.3-11
Psalm 118
Luke 24.1-12

Once again we are gathered to celebrate in story and symbol, in word and sacrament, the third and climactic moment in our celebration of the Christian Pasch.

In the story, we heard:

Darkness covered the face of the deep, while the Spirit of God swept over the face of the waters.

* * *

Moses stretched out his hand over the sea. The Lord drove the sea back by a strong east wind all night and turned the sea into dry land; and the waters were divide.

★ ★ ★

"O afflicted one, storm tossed and not comforted, I am about to … lay your foundations with sapphires. I will make your pinnacles of rubies, your gates of jewels, and all your walls of precious stones."

★ ★ ★

Do you not know that all of us who have been baptized into Christ Jesus were baptized into his death? Therefore we have been buried with him by baptism into death, so that, just as Christ was raised from the dead by the glory of the Father, so we too might walk in newness of life.

★ ★ ★

And now the ritual! Picture what we will be doing:

"Let your Spirit be upon the waters of this font"… "I baptize you in the name of the Father, and of the Son, and of the Holy Spirit."… "You have been called to fullness of life in water and the Holy Spirit. I anoint you with the chrism of salvation, fragrant oil that anoints prophets, priests, and kings. Take your place with them." "Be sealed with the gift of the Holy Spirit. Peace be with you."

Picture it! Anticipate its profound significance!

Pulled into the story, the newly baptized among us are drawn into the dignity and wonder of Christ's rising, into the paschal mystery, as are all of us who renew our baptismal vows and celebrate the mystery of our own rising with him.

I have a drawer in my desk where I put all kinds of stuff, clippings from papers and journals, poems and sayings that people send me. I should be more careful about noting the sources of these treasures. As time goes on, I can't remember where a lot of it came from.

The following was retrieved from that drawer. Where it comes from originally, I don't know, but it is said to have inspired parts of Nelson Mandela's inaugural address as President of South Africa:

Our deepest fear is not that we are inadequate;
our deepest fear is that we are powerful beyond measure.
It is our light, not our darkness that most frightens us.
We ask ourselves,
"Who am I to be brilliant, gorgeous, talented, and fabulous?"
Actually, who are you not to be?
You are a child of God.
Your playing small doesn't serve the world.
There is nothing enlightened about shrinking so that
People don't feel insecure around you.
We were born to make manifest the glory of God within us.
It is not just in some of us,
It's in everyone.
And, as we let our light shine,

We unconsciously give each other permission to do the same.
As we are liberated from our own fear,
Our presence liberates others.

What a wonderful Easter text! Isn't this what we are doing here, and what we are being here for each other? Isn't this what we were all about in the courtyard earlier, when, defying the mists of early spring, we lit a paschal fire?

Once again, in our paschal celebrations, we are "getting it right" here in church. We sense and believe that what we are doing here is "truly right and just." Once again, we do our liturgy with the confidence that the Spirit of the Risen Christ abides with us. We can do it out there, too. With grace and courage we can "get it right" as church—beyond these walls.

Look to the Holy of Holies

Easter Sunday

Acts 10.34a, 36-43
Psalm 118
Colossians 3.1-4
John 20.1-18

Before she met the Risen Jesus, whom she supposed was a gardener, Mary Magdalene bent into his tomb and saw two angels. They were seated on the shelf along the wall of the cave tomb. One sat at the head, the other at the foot, as if posed to bring to mind the Ark of the Covenant in the Holy of Holies—the place of ultimate meeting with God.

The presence of the angels was an invitation offered to her. "Why are you weeping?" they asked her. Even before she looked up and saw Jesus, she was being invited to discover him for herself by looking up, not down.

The presence of the angels revealed symbolically what Paul is getting at in the text from Colossians, which we have just heard: "If you have been raised with Christ, seek the things that are above, where Christ is seated at the right hand of God."

Look to the Holy of Holies, Paul is saying.

"Set your minds on things that are above, not on things that are on earth, for you have died, and your life is hidden with Christ in God."

As always, we have to look carefully at what Paul means when he is contrasting earth and heaven, world and spirit. He is talking about fundamental orientations, about looking down or looking up, about choosing death or life.

We get a taste of death when we live in bitterness, when prejudice blinds us to the truth, when loneliness enfolds us, when fears oppress

103

us, when sadness overwhelms us. In those moments the "world" closes in on us; we have one foot in the grave.

When we love and are loved, when we are accepted and accepting, when we are forgiven and forgiving, we are rising from the dead, heavenward in our orientation; we are Holy of Holies-bound.

The tensions implicit in our own life choices are clear. Our life stories are filled with examples of death-life choices, big and small.

Paul continues: "You have died, and your life is hidden with Christ in God. When Christ, who is your life, is revealed, then you also will be revealed with him in glory."

With Paul as background music, let's get back to the angels in the empty tomb. In one of my all-too-infrequent attempts to clean out my office and library, I came across Peter Berger's *A Rumor of Angels,* published in New York by Doubleday in 1969. It was pretty well-marked-up, so it must have been required reading for a course I was taking at the time at Saint Paul University.

Berger uses the concept of angel, traditionally a heavenly messenger, in an expanded or analogous way. In his book an angel is "a signal of the transcendent." That is to say, "a phenomenon that is to be found within the domain of our natural reality, but appears to point beyond that reality." Let's take a close look at Berger's angels.

The first is the *angel of trust.* A mother instinctively reassures her frightened little boy when he wakes up in the middle of the night. "Everything's going to be all right," she says as she holds him close. Is she lying? Naive? Or expressing a profound truth about the goodness and ultimate rightness of life? Is she not saying what Jesus himself believed as he was lifted on the cross and commended his spirit to God? "Jesus is risen," the angel of trust proclaims. Everything is going to be all right. Can you hear how this angel is speaking out of the empty tomb? "Why are you weeping?"

The second angel is the *angel of play.* She, too, is a signal of the transcendent. Little children play in the streets, they swim, they roller-blade. I remember how nervous my father used to get when he saw kids climbing trees. He could barely stand watching them. They seem to play in what Berger calls "direct defiance of the threat of death." The joy of play suspends or brackets death, and points exuberantly to the final victory of joy. This angel, too, is quite at home in the empty tomb, saying, "Why are you weeping?"

Berger's third angel is the *angel of hope*. At their best, people have a strong urge to say "No" when they are threatened. There is a tough streak in us, a stubborn, unyielding part of us that resists being wiped out or defeated even in the face of terror and danger. We all know people who simply refuse to get "down in the dumps" no matter what. As a priest, I've experienced this so often with sick and dying parishioners who have been such a wonderful example of hope and courage. Or consider the work of Mother Teresa against such great odds, or Nelson Mandela in prison for so many years. These people are either living some kind of delusion, or they are profoundly right. Even when life itself is threatened, there are people who rise up to say "No," even if the seemingly final outcome of their "No" is martyrdom. This angel, too, speaks out of the empty tomb. "Why are you weeping?"

The fourth is the *angel of humour*. For Berger, either laughter is an illusion or death is an illusion. How can you laugh if life is going to be snuffed out? Laughter is its own signal of transcendence. Death cannot be allowed to have the last laugh. Cynicism is the laughter of death. The real enjoyment of life in hearty laughter and celebration defies death and signals the ultimate victory of holiness. Did you see Roberto Benigni's wonderful film *Life Is Beautiful,* where a Jewish father "laughs his son to safety and freedom" in the midst of the Holocaust? "Why are you weeping?"

Jesus is risen! He is risen indeed! Let this quartet of Easter angels sing trust, play, hope and laughter into your hearts today. Let them direct your gaze to the Holy of Holies today. As you renew your baptismal vows and feel the springtime waters of rebirth sprinkled over you, affirm again your own commitment to life.

Glorious Wounds and Scars

Second Sunday of Easter

Acts 5.12–16
Psalm 118
Revelation 1.9–11a, 12–13, 17–19
John 20.19–31

Have you believed because you have seen me? Blessed are those who have not seen and yet have come to believe.

They were breathless—out of energy, full of fear. They had locked themselves up. The gospel says disciples, not apostles or the "twelve"—now eleven. How many would they have been, maybe more than twelve, maybe fewer? Men, women, Jesus' mother?

Whoever they were, they had good reason to lock themselves in on the first day of the week. It was the first day after the great Sabbath, when the authorities would have been free to pursue the followers of him whom they had crucified to make sure that the movement was over. Perhaps they would have been satisfied with negotiating their silence, or sending them back to Galilee where they came from, banning them from Jerusalem. Perhaps more drastic measures would have been taken—persecution, or even death. The political situation with the Romans was so precarious that there would be good reason for paranoia.

Then there was a breath. He just breezed through the door. The door was locked, but in he breezed. "Shalom. Peace be with you," and he breathed on them. Life would never be the same.

In Luke's book of Acts, it's a violent pentecostal wind and tongues of fire. In John it is breath emerging from the core of the Risen one. Do you remember how he died in Good Friday's gospel? "He bowed his head and gave up his spirit." He breathed his spirit upon the world.

Well, he's doing it again. The breath is being breathed, now from the Risen one. The Eternal word is speaking again—creating the universe anew—breathing a fresh start. As in Genesis 2, God is refashioning human beings from the dust of the earth, breathing life to make them "living persons."

We may not be used to seeing so much in such a brief text, but there it is, and what flows out of Jesus' breathing is even more amazing. There is breath here for the breathless. There is energy for the fearful, and do you notice the quality of the energy? Not for vindication, not for going to Pilate and saying I told you so, but for forgiveness of sins for those who would choose to be instruments of such a wonder. "Whose sins you shall forgive, they are forgiven."

But Thomas was not there. Preachers seem to like giving Thomas a hard time. Jesus says to him: "Have you believed because you have seen me? Blessed are those who have not seen and yet have come to believe."

Let's take another look and at least give Thomas credit for asking the right questions, looking for the right "proofs." He wants to see the wounds. He wants to be in touch with the wounds. Thomas wants to be sure that there is real continuity between the Jesus he knew and touched and the "Risen Christ" who breezes through doors. If the wounded one is risen, Thomas will be ready for his own set of wounds, and will be ready to let his own wounds serve the faith of others.

Thomas leaves us with this test, which he imposed upon his Lord, and it's a good one. It is the test that has value down through the ages. It is a test of authenticity, of genuine witness to faith.

"Are you a Christian, my friend? Please, may I see your hands; may I see your feet; may I see your side?" If you find wounds in your friend, glorious wounds and scars, you'll know that she's for real, that she really cares about the justice, honesty and integrity for which Jesus lived and died. Risen beyond her own struggles, she too can say "Peace," and breathe life into your doubts.

In the Book of Revelation, Jesus takes the initiative and stretches out his wounded hand. John was "in the Spirit on the Lord's Day" and felt the touch of his hand and heard him saying: "Do not be afraid; I am the first and the last, and the living one. I was dead, but see, I am alive forever and ever; and I have the keys of death and of Hades."

In the Spirit on this Lord's Day, we bear the same message to each other. In this Easter eucharist, we extend wounded hands as we greet each other in the peace of Christ. We extend these same wounded hands as we say "Amen" to the Body of Christ broken for our peace.

Shepherding Each Other

Third Sunday of Easter

Acts 5.27-32, 40b-41
Psalm 30
Revelation 5.11-14
John 21.1-19

Next Sunday is "Good Shepherd" Sunday, which centres on the shepherding role of Jesus as he gathers, nurtures and protects his flock.

Today we celebrate another kind of Good Shepherd Sunday, which focuses on the shepherding to which Peter is called. His three-fold denial of Jesus is not held against him as he is challenged three times to profess his love and invited three times to share in the ministry of the Risen Jesus. "Feed my lambs. Tend my lambs. Feed my sheep. Follow me."

There's no indication that the project will be an easy one. "Very truly, I tell you, when you were younger, you used to fasten your own belt and go wherever you wished. But when you grow old, you will stretch out your hands, and someone else will fasten a belt around you and take you where you do not wish to go."

Of course, the first level of interpretation refers to Peter directly. Jesus says this to "indicate the kind of death by which he would glorify God." We have also gotten used to thinking about the text as subsequently referring to the ministry of the pope, or even pastors of local churches.

Last Sunday one of our senior members who participates regularly in either the 9:30 or 11:00 liturgy was commenting on "how busy these Easter Masses are." Baptisms, First Communions, witness talks by young people preparing for confirmation ... "We have a busy flock here," she said. She was delighted that we were making such a "fuss" over the children and had just given a big hug to a mother, who had a toddler already in tow, who had presented her newborn daughter for baptism. Needless to say, I was delighted with her response, and especially pleased with the operative word "we." "*We* have a busy flock here, and it is wonderful that *we* are making a 'fuss' over *our* children."

During Lent, many of you "adopted" children and committed yourselves to be their prayer partners as they prepared for First Communion and Confirmation. I hope that you have been faithful to your prayer and will take the time to prepare a card or a note when their special day comes.

Even as sheep, members of the flock of Christ, we become shepherds for each other as we follow him. Following Jesus makes us all shepherds. As members of a community and co-responsible for one another, we don't just "fasten our own belts and go where we want." Sometimes, we're led even where we would not otherwise wish to go as we nurture, tend and feed each other. Perhaps no one knows better than parents how that experience feels.

I've told you before about my drawer full of clippings, poems, bits and pieces that I have found or that have been given to me over the years. I'm going to read a prayer that comes out of that drawer. Instead of or in addition to the general intercessions, or prayers of the people which we offer each Sunday, some churches have a longer "pastoral prayer," which is prepared by and offered by the pastor and reflects what is being read or celebrated at a particular service. During this prayer, the congregation is customarily seated with heads bowed, even eyes closed.

As I offer this prayer, think of Alexander, who will be baptized at this liturgy, or one of the children making their First Communion today, or one of your own children or grandchildren, a niece or nephew, sibling or cousin. Picture a particular child; pray with me for her; shepherd him in your heart. You may even wish to bow your heads and close your eyes.

Lord God, our Father,
You have given your Son, Jesus Christ, to us as the good shepherd
Who knows us all by name.

We thank you
for your grace and faithfulness to our human families,
for the new life that you have created,
for this child who has been born among us
and whom you have entrusted to our care.
You have given him eyes to see with
and ears to hear with.
Bless too this child's mouth,
so that he may learn to laugh
and to communicate with others.
Bless also her hands and feet
and may he learn from his experience
that everything that you have made is good.
We ask you to shelter this child
and to make him safe in this rough world.
Keep everything that is bad and inhuman away from him;
protect him from all harm.
May he be secure with his family
and may all who are mature and responsible
never give scandal to this little one,
but lead him to the truth in love.
If, however, sin should ever have power over him,
be merciful to him, Lord God—
You make good all human guilt and shortcomings
and are yourself,
even before this child came into the world,
infinite mercy and compassion
in Jesus Christ, our Lord.
Amen.

Cleansed in the Blood of the Lamb

Fourth Sunday of Easter

Acts 13.14, 43-52
Psalm 100
Revelation 7.9, 14b-17
John 10.27-30

Children are probably more in touch with the fact that the imagination, with its wild and crazy images, can sometimes communicate truth better than straight talk. Today's text from the Book of Revelation is a good example: a wonderful dream, a wonderful set of images needs to capture and fascinate our imaginations and our whole being—even though we might want to avoid the pull of these images. Here is the picture the writer paints: a great multitude of people, so many that no one can count them; people from every nation, all tribes, all languages, all ways of life, standing together around the throne of God. They are robed in white and waving palm branches. These are the people who have washed their robes in the blood of the lamb of God. Singing, they gather around his throne day and night. There's no more hunger, no more famine, no more scorching heat—just springs of life and water, and no more tears. And on the throne, a lamb, pierced for our sins.

Some people don't want to be part of that world. Do we really want to be a part of a world where black people, white people, oriental people and native people all sit at the same table singing the same song? Are we going to be happy when we get to heaven and find out that this is the way it will be for ever and ever?

In her address on the occasion of the fiftieth anniversary of the end of the Second World War, Queen Elizabeth spoke about the high ideals that motivated those who shed their blood during that great conflict. She also pointed to the same old stuff in our world today: the same kinds of divisions and alienation in places like Croatia and Serbia, where the same old conflicts bubble up over and over again. That doesn't apply only to the Balkans. Even here in Canada, political leaders seem to find it necessary on occasion to call each other pro-vocative names like "traitor," which doesn't promote the process of healing, reconciling and unifying people.

Right down the street the other day we had a mini rumble between students of the Catholic high school and the public high school. This is more of the same old stuff for which there is absolutely no excuse. Crowds of people from many nations, washed in the blood of the lamb: the great vision of the Book of Revelation tells us that this is how it will be in God's kingdom. We might as well get used to it and start building it today, because God is going to make it happen. God will make reconciliation real, true and permanent, so we might as well get used to it now.

Consider the wonderful image of the lamb. It portrays the rite of the ancient covenant in which the spring lamb was slaughtered and shared by the people. Its blood was sprinkled upon the congregation and the altar, signifying communion in blood between God and the people, as well as purification of sin, selfishness, division, alienation. The great communion of the ancient covenant in the blood of sacri-fice, the spring paschal sacrifice: this is Jesus, whose body is broken and given for us. We are cleansed in the blood of the lamb that we share in this place. That's the truth. That's how we'll live forever around the throne of the lamb of God.

Yet we're so easily distracted. We so easily find ourselves retreating into our own little territories just like cats, clinging to our own turf. Someday that will all be gone. Let's get used to it and let it go—now. The Book of Revelation holds out the truth of God's great plan for us. It invites us even now to get with the program, because nothing else will last anyway. We celebrate that great wonder in communion at this altar, at this table where we gather every week—and some of us every day. We say "Amen" to the lamb broken and given for our communion, for our reconciliation. Our eucharist constantly invites us to put all pettiness and disorder aside in favour of the love of God that we celebrate here in a profound and beautiful way as we receive these children to our table for the first time. We pray that we might be worthy to invite them to participate in our life and that our life may be true, transparent, open.

"This is the lamb of God": in just a few moments we'll be saying those words to these beautiful children who are making their First Communion. Look at them: they represent all the great races, tribes, cultures and colours of the world, gathered right here in our own church, singing the same song and being open to the lamb of God.

The Maternal Side

Fifth Sunday of Easter

Acts 14.21b-27
Psalm 145
Revelation 21.1-5a
John 13.1, 31-33a, 34-35

The texts chosen for today's liturgy, the Fifth Sunday of Easter, really have nothing to do with Mother's Day, but I found myself reading them with Mother's Day in mind. In fact, there is a great coincidence, an underlying connection between them and Mother's Day. The texts deal with actions and attitudes.

The first text deals with the actions and attitudes of the first apostles. What are they doing? They are strengthening the souls of the others. They're encouraging them to continue in their faith. They are praying for them. This is the maternal side of being an apostle, the maternal side of ministry: the encouragement, the prayer, the strengthening of the soul. For most of us, who has been the person who strengthened and encouraged our development in faith and in prayer?

The psalm and the second reading reflect the maternal side of God: the Lord is gracious, the Lord is merciful, the Lord is reconciling, the Lord is slow to anger and abounding in love, the Lord is compassion over all that is made. The text from Revelation speaks of wiping tears from people's eyes, announcing that mourning and crying can pass, announcing that something can be new, that healing can take place, that everything is going to be okay—because God is alive. This is the maternal side of God and Jesus: "Little children, love one another. Don't let anything separate you from one another. Don't let anything tear you apart. Love one another. Be faithful and generous to each other. Love one another as I love you." This is the maternal side of Jesus, who prays as he comes into Jerusalem that he will be able to gather all of these straying people like little chicks under the mother's wings.

This is the maternal side of the apostolate, the maternal side of God, the maternal side of Jesus. Most of us have experienced it in our own lives in the ministry of women—our mothers and our grandmothers. In my own life, a number of religious sisters who taught me when I was a very young boy were wonderful signs of gentleness and compassion and encouragement in faith and in hope.

These texts, even though they have nothing explicitly to do with Mother's Day, invite us to bless and praise God for the ways in which we have been nourished, encouraged and sustained in mind and heart through our life of faith, through our life in the community. While this compassionate nurturing is not just a mother's work, it is in the maternal side of God reflected in the ministry which women have always offered to Christian believers that we have experienced this aspect of God's way of being. The ministry of women, the ministry of women at home, in prayer, in their own unique way of being leaders in our community is something for which we can be thankful. It's something to celebrate, not just on Mother's Day, but as part of the wonderful heritage of the Christian church.

Pneumatic Energy

Sixth Sunday of Easter

Acts 15.1–2, 22–29
Psalm 67
Revelation 21.10–14, 22–23
John 14.23–29

"Those who love me will keep my word, and my Father will love them, and we will come to them and make our home with them …. The Advocate, the Holy Spirit … will teach you everything."
"It has seemed good to the Holy Spirit, and to us, to impose on you no further burden than these essentials."

There is a wonderful story of an old rabbi who was working with a group of young children, reflecting on the beautiful Psalm 139:

O Lord, you have probed me. You know me.
You know me when I sit and when I stand.
You know everything about me.
Even as I was being knit together in my mother's womb you were there;
the wonderful knitting together of all my parts,
the wonder of my body, the wonder of my person.

The rabbi was reflecting on that beautiful text about the wonderful knitting together of all their parts, and asked the children what part they thought was most important. One little girl said, "Well, it's the lungs, because if we stop breathing, we stop living." Someone else said, "No it's the heart, because if the heart stops beating and pumping the blood all around, you stop living." Somebody else said, "No, it's the stomach, because if you stop eating you are just going to shrivel up and be nothing." Some very smart little person said, "No, it's the brain, because the brain signals the lungs and the heart and the stomach. It's the brain that's the most important."

And the rabbi said, "No, I'm talking about the person, not the body. What's the most important part of the person?" And they didn't know. The rabbi said, "It's a tube that goes from your senses to your soul and back. It's through that tube that you decide when to laugh, when to cry. It's through that tube, the tube between the senses, the eyes and the ears and the smell and the touch and the soul, that you decide how to be compassionate and gentle and loving and courageous. God's blowing in that tube."

The tube might seem like a strange way of expressing it, but it sounds to me as though the rabbi was getting at the "nervous system," which keeps the whole body co-ordinated and sensitive, and I would hope sensible as well. At any rate, the most important part is that which keeps all the parts working together. The most important characteristic of a person is that he or she is whole, well integrated, well put together, playing with a full deck of cards.

A similar tradition lies behind what Jesus is saying about sending this new breath, this new Spirit, this new advocate, the new connector or integrator of persons and communities. This Spirit will speak in the connections, in the lifelines connecting persons, in the central nervous system of a community of faith. When the community gathers, the Spirit, the advocate, the teacher is among and in between—in the "tubes," in the "lines." The Spirit of the Risen Jesus as advocate heightens communication, seals solidarity, and establishes communion among all related parts of the Body of Christ.

"It seems good to the Holy Spirit and to us ...." When Christians gather in the Spirit (the advocate), they are reminded of what matters most to Jesus. Jesus' cause is pleaded among and between them in their discernment.

Let me give you a good example: our pastoral council, at the invitation of Catholic Immigration Services and the archbishop, is considering the Bosnian family project which you have already heard about. Is this "do-able"? Is it worthwhile? A lot of people in our culture and our society will say that there are too many refugees and immigrants already. All you're doing is setting somebody else up for the welfare rolls. There are further considerations about race and religion. But we don't make a decision based on just that. There are surely bad reasons not to jump in. There may also be very good reasons not to take this on and to invest our resources and energies elsewhere. We need to try to be open, to move beyond ourselves, to the breath of the Spirit, to the electricity of love and generosity at work among us and between us until with confidence we can say: "It seems good to the Holy Spirit and to us."

The problem faced by the early church reflected in today's text from Acts is another good example. Coincidentally enough, it too was about "adopting" outsiders. What do you do with the Gentiles? People from all different groups were coming into the Christian religion; they were not rooted in the traditions of Moses; they had not been Jews first. What is required of them?

Note the conclusion of their discernment which was formulated into a letter to the community. "It has seemed good to the Holy Spirit and to us to impose on you Gentiles no further burden than these essentials." To us today the essentials seem very strange: abstain from what has been sacrificed to idols, from blood, from what is strangled and from fornication. "If you keep yourselves from these, you will do well."

What about their conclusions? They sound strange, don't they? We can easily see that to abstain from fornication is a reasonable expectation about family, commitment and loyalty, but what makes those other ones so essential? Well, if the Gentiles observe these minimal dietary restrictions, the Jewish Christians would still be able to eat with them, even if they're still observing all their ancestral kosher and ritual traditions. These minimal dietary restrictions are essential to table fellowship, which is so key in Luke's gospel. They are essential to communion, ultimately to sharing the eucharist.

Since the first generation of the church, the Father and Son, in the Spirit, have made their home with Christian communities, with those who love and strive to keep God's word. Energized by and united in that kind of spiritual electricity, that kind of "pneumatic energy," individuals, families and communities can be confident in their prayerfully-made life decisions.

"Come, Holy Spirit. Fill the hearts of your faithful. Enkindle in them the fire of your love."

Out!

Ascension

Acts 1.1-11
Psalm 47
Hebrews 9.24-28; 10.19-23
Luke 24.46-53

The women were standing there gazing into the empty tomb. While they were perplexed about this, suddenly two men in dazzling clothes stood beside them. The women were terrified and bowed their faces to the ground, but the men said to them, "Why do you look for the living among the dead?" (Luke 24:4)

While he was going and they were gazing up toward heaven, suddenly two men in white robes stood by them. They said, "Men of Galilee, why do you stand looking up toward heaven?" (Acts 1:10-11a)

Where's a person supposed to look? If not down, and not up, then where?

The forty days between resurrection and ascension represents a serious number: fullness of time, plenty of time for the men and women who were his disciples to probe the mystery. Jewish students study with a rabbi for forty days, a symbolic number meaning the amount of time it would take to learn the master's teaching well enough to repeat it.

The ascension event is told in a way that is full of allusions to biblical precedents. Being lifted up before their eyes into the cloud refers to the cloud of God's presence, which went before the people of Israel leading them through the wilderness to freedom. By being gathered into the cloud, Jesus is not so much going up as he is going ahead of his apostles into glory. To ask astrophysical questions about where Jesus was headed and what propelled him is to get it all mixed up and to miss the ascension's essential sense of direction.

On Easter the women were told not to look down into the tomb; now the apostles are told not to look into the heavens. "Beginning from Jerusalem you are witnesses," Jesus said. "I am sending upon you what my Father promised…. You will be clothed with power from on high." The issue is not where Jesus was, or even where he is, but where he is sending them, clothed with power from on high. The direction is not down or up, but *out*. They are no longer only hearers of the word, but its heralds.

Do you remember another mountain, the mount of transfiguration, which we visited on the Second Sunday of Lent? "While he was praying, the appearance of his face changed, and his clothes became dazzling white. Suddenly they [Peter, James and John] saw two men, Moses and Elijah, talking to Jesus. They appeared in glory and were speaking of his departure, which he was about to accomplish in Jerusalem."

The scholarly commentaries to which I have been referring during this Year of Luke do not make an explicit connection between the transfiguration and the resurrection–ascension event, or between Moses and Elijah, the two men at the tomb, and the two men at Bethany, but I have a funny feeling that there may be such a connection.

Both Moses and Elijah know what "passing the torch" is all about. When Moses died and was buried (although nobody could ever find his grave), Joshua took over. The staff of God, which opened the way of promise, was now in his hands. Before Elijah was taken to heaven in a chariot of fire, his successor, Elisha, asked for a double share of his spirit. Clothed with Elijah's mantle, he continued his mission mightily.

The ascension story serves as the hinge of a diptych—a two-panelled image joined in the middle. Luke's gospel is one panel; the Acts of the Apostles is the other panel. As we move through the ascension experience, Luke's point of view changes. The issues change. We move, as it were, from the story of Jesus to the story of the Church, from then to now. In the ascension story, the staff of Jesus is passed.

"Clothed with power from on high," clothed with his mantle, the disciples are charged with the continuation of his mission.

The gospel of Luke tells of the disciples' journey toward faith in Jesus. The ascension, a hinge moment, reflects something new, which the Acts of the Apostles will carry forward even to our own time and beyond.

The issue in this hinge moment is not so much our faith in Jesus, as Jesus' faith in us.

The issue is not our giving his resurrection a certificate of authenticity, but his decision to pour out his spirit upon struggling believers.

The issue is not for us to prove that Jesus is alive, but for him to prove that we are not dead.

The issue is no longer his identity with God, but our identity with him.

Do you feel a bit shaky at times as you face your own life with all of its ambiguities? The mystery of the ascension invites us, even in our shakiness, not so much to believe in God, but to believe that God believes in us. In other words: don't get stuck looking down in discouragement, or looking up in bewilderment. Staff in hand, mantle around your shoulders, look out and step out with grace and courage.

A Fiftieth Day of Our Own

Pentecost Sunday

Acts 2.1-11
Psalm 104
Romans 8.8-17
John 14.15-16, 23b-26

We celebrated confirmation with about thirty of our young people just a few weeks ago. As part of the retreat preparing for confirmation, we were going over the rite, especially the profession of faith that they would be making in the presence of the bishop and the whole assembly.

I reminded them that as part of their profession of faith, the bishop would be asking: "Do you believe in the Holy Spirit, the Lord, the giver of life, who came upon the apostles at Pentecost and today is given to you sacramentally in confirmation?" They would respond: "I do."

They knew quite a lot about Pentecost. They knew that it came fifty days after Easter. I explained to them that there were seven days in the week, which in the Bible became a symbol for fullness. They knew that 7 times 7 equals 49 plus 1 is 50, and had fun figuring out what the significance of that "Pentecost number" might be. It didn't take long for them to decide that fullness times fullness equals "overflow": something new, exciting and wonderful.

You will remember from the text of Acts, which we heard last Sunday, that Jesus' last instruction to his disciples was to wait in Jerusalem until they should be baptized with the Holy Spirit, and that his last promise to them was, "You will receive power when the Holy Spirit comes upon you: and you will bear witness for me in Jerusalem, and all over Judea and Samaria, to the ends of the earth."

The roaring wind out of the sky and the tongues of fire on this fiftieth day are clearly important, and the boys and girls seemed to enjoy imagining the scene.

In the Bible, wind and spirit are closely related. The idea of breath brings out their divine connection even further. Breath, wind and spirit are all about life and energy. The children had seen pictures of a newborn baby held upside-down and given a "spank" so that she would catch her breath and live in a new way. In creating the first human, God was pictured in the book of Genesis as taking dust from the earth and breathing life into it. The great wind coming from the sky with such force was the breath of God inviting the whole world to catch its breath and be born again. It was the breath of God for the re-creation of the world.

The tongues of fire are interesting, too. Fire, with its immense capacity for constructive and destructive uses, is another traditional symbol for divine energy. Steel is purified and refined in a furnace. We speak of being on fire when we are in love or are deeply committed to something. God's work among us is refining, purifying and energizing for love and service.

So far, so good, but we have to move beyond those poetic biblical images to the twenty-first-century concreteness of our own lives. It's easier to explain the richness of the Pentecost story to a confirmation class, and more difficult to come to terms with its projected outcomes for their lives.

> Do *you* believe in the Holy Spirit?
> Are *you* in touch with the Lord, the Giver of life?
> Is there wind blowing in *you*?
> Is there fire energizing *you*?

Moving to this level with the twelve-year-old confirmation candidates was more difficult. It was not easy for them to imagine that this same Holy Spirit, which was poured out in Jerusalem so long ago, was available to them, in their lives, which seem quite ordinary.

In the celebration of confirmation, the bishop rubbed the perfumed oil (holy chrism) into their heads in the shape of the cross. "Be sealed with the gift of the Holy Spirit." "Peace be with you," he breathed upon them. The Holy Spirit is not given "in general," or for the disciples way back then, but for these young people today.

The confirmation class is not alone in finding this difficult. It's easier for all of us to come to terms with the meaning of a "way-back-then Pentecost," and more difficult to come to terms with living a fiftieth day of our own.

What can you name in your own life that needs purification or refinement? Or what in your life is in the process of being purified and refined? What needs energy and fire, or is currently being energized and heated up? Can you recognize and name the Holy Spirit's wind and fire in these real-life challenges and experiences?

A few years ago, after the archbishop's annual invitation to a special wedding anniversary Mass at the cathedral for people married twenty-five or fifty years, a couple stopped me after Mass and wanted to come in to see me. They came the following evening, and asked if they could go to that Mass even though they had only been married for four years. They had come through a very hard time, had sought counselling, and really believed that they were back on track. They wanted to renew their vows. Of course you can go, I said. We talked further and prayed together, celebrating the sacrament of reconciliation. They were sure that it was God who had kept them together. They went to the cathedral and felt "sealed" with the gift of a renewing Spirit, an energizing, refining Spirit.

In the beginning of his book *Eternal Echoes* (New York: Harper Collins, 1999, p. xxvii), John O'Donohue offers a more general example of an area of contemporary life that calls out for purification, refinement and energizing with a breath of fresh air. He writes:

> Many of the really powerful forces in contemporary culture work to seduce human longing along the path of false satisfaction. When our longing becomes numbed, our sense of satisfaction becomes empty and cold; this intensifies the sense of isolation and distance that so many people now feel. Consumerism is the worship of the god of quantity; advertising is its liturgy. Advertising is schooling in false longing. More and more the world of image claims our longing. Image is mere surface veneer. It is no wonder that there is such a crisis of

belonging now since there is no homeland in this external world of image and product. It is a famine field of the Spirit. Despite all the energy and development that have taken place, many areas in modern life are losing their nature and grace.

"Human longing and false satisfaction; emptiness and cold; god of quantity; living on the surface; world of image and product; life losing grace...." Do you feel these pressures in your own life, in your family's life, or in your children's lives? I do. Do you feel the need for a refining, energizing spirit to build and develop fullness, warmth, quality, depth and grace that would be truly satisfying and ennobling of people? I do.

We may not hear a rushing Pentecostal wind, but the Spirit is here, available to the faithful. As we pray and sing together in this liturgy, let's breathe deeply.

"Come, Holy Spirit. Fill the hearts of your faithful. Enkindle in them the fire of your love."

God as Plural

Trinity Sunday

Proverbs 8.22-31
Psalm 8
Romans 5.1-5
John 16.12-15

The Blessed Trinity! Some of us will remember how, even as children, we wondered about a father and son being coeternal and a Holy Spirit being a person—at least I did. Some of us may remember as well how the Holy Trinity was pictured as a triangle: three equal sides, one shape, or, thanks to St. Patrick, as a cloverleaf or shamrock: three leaves on one stem. I remember especially the triangle which was painted on the wall of a church near home. It had a big eye in the middle of it. I see some of you nodding, so you must be at least as old as I am to remember that kind of symbolism in church decoration! We've all seen St. Patrick with a cloverleaf in his hand.

The scriptures that we have just heard don't use the language of the Nicene Creed, nor do they use the symbols that were on the church walls of my childhood. Instead, they invite us to pay attention to the ways in which we experience the Spirit of God at work in creation, in history and in our own personal lives.

The first reading wonders at the universe and recognizes that there is a creative process at work under the guidance of a master builder. Divine wisdom is rejoicing before God as the universe takes shape, finding particular delight in us humans. The Spirit is at work in creation.

The second reading recognizes Our Lord Jesus Christ as source of the Spirit for enduring the sufferings and tensions that bring us to true life. The Spirit is at work in the life, death and resurrection of Jesus.

The gospel describes Jesus' promise of the Spirit who will dwell in the depths of the human spirit guiding persons in the way of his own truth and life. The Spirit is at work in the depths of our own conscience as we live in faith from day to day.

I don't want to oversimplify things, but there seems to be a threefold way in which God is experienced by persons open to faith.

The wonder of a new day, or the wonder of a whole new world in its springtime rebirth. The wonder of the stars in heaven, or the wonder of the birth of a child—or even of a mosquito as you watch her biting you—invites your imagination to soar to the Source of all that is, the Creator of the Universe whom Jesus calls Father. *God is present in creation.*

When I was chaplain at Immaculata High School in Ottawa, we took a busload of students to Toronto to meet and hear Mother Teresa and Jean Vanier. After they spoke, one of the girls said, "I was listening to God." Her reaction signals "incarnation." *God is present in history.* God can speak in human history. Christians acknowledge that presence uniquely in Jesus, whom we call the Christ.

We also meet and discover God in our own "dream world," in our own conscience, or in the funny ways in which we intuit certain things. We've all had experiences that we simply cannot explain, when God's Spirit seems to jump inside us, when we get some kind of insight, or when our conscience bugs us. *God is present in the depths of our being.*

If I remember correctly, this threefold way in which God can be experienced was called "Modalism" in the early centuries of the church and condemned as heresy. God is not simply experienced in three different ways or modes. God is three persons.

Just after Easter, I was at St. Benoît du Lac near Magog, Quebec, for a short retreat. It's worth a trip there, even for a visit. The abbey is a daughter abbey of Solesmes in France, famous for the study and preservation of Gregorian Chant. At St. Benoît, the liturgy is celebrated in French, but the music is largely the traditional Latin chant, which is not only beautiful but prayerful in a unique way.

In the guest library, I was given a copy of *Wonder and Poverty* by Maurice Zundel. It was a set of conferences given to a group of cloistered nuns in Switzerland. One of the chapters discussed the Trinity, and if you can imagine, it was very interesting.

Zundel asked, "What if God is single?" God is one—but what if God is single? He went on to show how easy it is to distort the concept of one God and make it into not only a male figure, but into a kind of colossus—a pharoah, a Ramses II deified. To do so would be to distort the I AM WHO I AM that is God's revealed name, and to make God into a power—however benevolent—over and against all that is.

The power of I AM WHO I AM is *love*. If God is love, Zundel suggests, God must in some way be plural or interpersonal. If God is two, then two persons loving each other that intensely and that indefinitely would turn in upon themselves in an exclusive way, which would not be Love. God has to be three. If God were four, God would be two couples.

That God is three suggests that there is no possibility of being a pharoah, exercising power in monstrous ways, nor is there possibility of the so-called love which is exclusive and self-serving.

Suggesting the famous icon that we have hanging in the narthex, God is three lovers, bending towards each other. God is self-emptying mystery into which we are invited.

Pretty abstract, isn't it? But do you see what he's trying to say? If the nature of God is love, Zundel suggests, God cannot be one. Nor can God be two—however co-equal and divine—that's too introverted and exclusive. God is *three*.

God is One. God is Personal. God is Love. God is Three.

He suggests that the number three represents a dynamic of self-emptying, essential to community. God is not static, but dynamic. The essence of God is not power, but love; not perfection, but compassion. God is one, but God is not single. God is Love. God is Three.

The reason I'm sharing my understanding of Zundel's insight is not to explain the Trinity, but to demonstrate how clearly our traditional Trinitarian theology invites us beyond an image of God as distant power or "old man in the sky." Zundel's "trio of lovers" does not answer all the questions, but it does invite us into the mystery of love and mutuality—solidarity and communion—which he suggests characterizes God's very being.

How appropriate, then, is the communion hymn we will sing today: "God is love, and we, who abide in Love, abide in God, and God in us."

One Body,
One Holy Communion

The Body and Blood of Christ

Genesis 14.18-20
Psalm 110
1 Corinthians 11.23-26
Luke 9.11b-17

Corpus Christi is the Latin name for the feast that we celebrate today. *Corpus Christi* means simply "the body of Christ." Let's spend a few minutes probing that mystery, probing those words which have become so common for us who come forward for communion regularly.

In a famous homily (242), St. Augustine notes the procedure for coming forward for communion in his own time, and asks the assembly to take special note of what it is that they are doing and saying.

The people are in procession, coming forward with open hands. In presenting a morsel of bread, the minister proclaims in faith: *"Corpus Christi."* The communicant responds in faith: "Amen."

Augustine comments: "It is your sacrament which you receive. You answer 'Amen' to what you yourself are and in answering you are enrolled. You answer 'Amen' to the words 'The Body of Christ.' Be, then, a member of the body to verify your 'Amen.'"

Think of it! It's one thing to recognize the "real presence" of Jesus in the bread and wine of the altar. It is another thing to recognize your own presence in that same bread and wine, to believe and affirm that you are a member of Christ; that *we* are the Body of Christ.

Augustine is inviting us to make those connections, to celebrate the mystery of Christ's presence—and what a mystery it is. To close

132

our eyes and to commune with Jesus is one thing; to commune in the Body of Christ is more complex, and may require even more faith.

Augustine is inviting us to open our eyes and to recognize that in the eucharist we are being drawn into communion with each other. We believe in Jesus; we believe in each other. We affirm Jesus; we affirm each other. We feed on Jesus; we feed on each other ... all of this in spite of our quirks, failings, weaknesses and sins.

When we affirm and celebrate the "body of Christ," we are engaged in an act of faith and of hope. Being able to say "Amen" to the body of Christ in all the richness of that image is clearly a work in progress for our own faith assembly and for the whole church. It is the work of the Spirit.

I'm sure you've noticed how this works in the eucharistic prayer.

In just a few moments we will pray: "Let your spirit come upon these gifts to make them holy, so that they may become for us the body and blood of your Son, Our Lord, Jesus Christ, at whose command we celebrate this eucharist," and later, "Grant that we who are nourished by his body and blood may be filled with his Holy Spirit and become one body, one spirit in him."

Clearly, Augustine is doing nothing more than commenting on the expansive faith content implicit in "The Body of Christ." "Amen."

To recognize the presence of Christ in a morsel of bread, in myself, in each other, in the historic church requires deep faith—and hope ... a big "Amen."

I was visiting with a colleague a couple of weeks ago. He had given a lot of energy to faith, religion and church over the years, but was at the point of crisis. Very discouraged by scandals in the church, bewildered by official positions and pronouncements, he confessed his temptation just to get out, to "leave it alone," to imitate Jesus in his own way, to find his own spiritual path apart from the organization. After further conversation, his position mellowed, but he was clearly in pain. I wish I had thought to give it to him then, but I later sent him a copy of a text to which I have returned over the years. It is part of the commencement address given by Walter Burghardt, the eminent Jesuit theologian and preacher, at Saint Mary's Seminary in Baltimore in 1970. Imagine—thirty years ago! Although not discussing the eucharist explicitly, he was clearly dealing with the "body of Christ." Listen to what he said:

> In the course of a half century, I have seen more Christian corruption than you have read of. I have tasted it. I have been reasonably corrupt myself. And yet, I love this Church, this living, pulsing, sinning people of God with a crucifying passion. Why? For all the Christian hate, I experience here a community of love. For all the institutional idiocy, I find here a tradition of reason. For all the individual repressions, I breath here an air of freedom. For all the fear of sex, I discover here the redemption of my body. In an age so inhuman, I touch here tears of compassion. In a world so grim and humourless, I share here rich joy and earthy laughter. In the midst of death, I hear here an incomparable stress on life. For all the apparent absence of God, I sense here the real presence of Christ.

Strong words, aren't they? Faith in the real presence stretches beyond eucharistic elements.

To celebrate the eucharist implies communion with and fidelity to the body of Christ in all of its dimensions. Faith in the eucharist includes humble hopefulness. It demands that in faith and hope we identify with and engage ourselves in all the active verbs which Burghardt uses: tasting, loving, experiencing, finding, breathing, discovering, touching, sharing, hearing, sensing the real presence of Christ in word, sacrament, community, history, all of life.

"Corpus Christi." "The Body of Christ."

Answer 'Amen' to that which you eat and drink, and to that which *you* are, to that which *we* are, and are called to become.

Tearless Faces

Eleventh Sunday in Ordinary Time

2 Samuel 12.7-10, 13
Psalm 32
Galatians 2.16, 19-21
Luke 7.36–8.3

As is the case with so many of history's big players, and I suppose with most of us lesser players, too, each story conceals a place of shadows.

Today's text is taken from one of the Bible's most wonderfully worked narratives. It is the story of David, the best-remembered of Israel's kings, who is in many ways idealized as a super-hero. Yet there is nothing heroic about this part of his story. You will remember how, as king, he seems to have distanced himself from battle, letting the others do the fighting; how he lusted after Bathsheba, committed adultery with her, and then sent for her husband, and tried to get them together so that nobody would know that there was anything unusual about her pregnancy. His plan failed because Uriah the Hittite refused to go home as long as his comrades were still in battle. So far David stands condemned on two counts. He subsequently arranged for Uriah to be sent to the front lines where his death would be inevitable—the third count. Uriah was killed as planned, and David took Bathsheba as one of his wives. So, did he then live happily ever after? Not quite. After David pretends to others and to himself that nothing had happened, the prophet Nathan enters the scene and tells David a powerful story.

Nathan told the story far more elegantly than this, but here's my quick version for today—by all means, read the original in 2 Samuel.

A man had a whole flock of sheep and was very rich. Another man had only one little lamb, whom he treated almost as a child. One day the rich man spotted that lamb. Maybe because of the special attention, it was just a bit fatter (better built) or more "table ready" than any of his. Anyway, he stole it from the poor man and had it for lunch. "What do you think of that?" Nathan asked.

"I'd take that son of a gun and string him up," David answered. "You are that man," concluded Nathan. Today's text continues their dialogue.

David got the message and confessed his sins to Nathan. All we have in the text is:

"David said to Nathan: 'I have sinned against the Lord.' Nathan said to David, 'Now the Lord has put away your sin; you shall not die.'"

What we don't have in today's text is God's word about the consequences of sin, about the fact that although David will be freed from death, his son born to Uriah's wife will not. We hear nothing of David's pleading and see nothing of his tears of pain and regret that are traditionally reflected in Psalm 51. Nor do we hear about God's great act of reconciliation, which is the birth of a second son to David and Bathsheba, the great King Solomon.

It is almost as if the gospel takes up where the David story leaves off. The woman's extravagant witness to the reality of sin, the pain it causes, the need to pour out one's heart, and the possibility of forgiveness and renewal are clearly and powerfully evident in both the witness of David and this unnamed woman.

Faith saves; freedom and peace are possible. But, did you notice, the tears come *after* the forgiveness, not before? Nathan announces that David's sins are forgiven. Only then does David respond with his prayers, tears and fasting, which reflect profound possibilities of change and renewal.

Jesus notes that this woman's sins—her many sins—have been forgiven; her perfumed tears poured out upon his feet reflect her sense of that reality.

It is with loving tears that both David and the woman of the gospel move on. It is clear, both in David the Old Testament super-hero and in the unnamed woman of the gospel, that forgiveness is not a reward for tears. Their tears are a sign of their experience of forgiveness and their loving embrace of that experience.

By the way, what makes Simon, at the head of the table, so problematic for Jesus? Why, in Luke's telling of the story, does Jesus find him and others like him so difficult to deal with? May I make a suggestion? It is the sin that their tearless faces seek to hide.

Embracing the Cross

Twelfth Sunday in Ordinary Time

Zechariah 12.10-11
Psalm 63
Galatians 3.26-29
Luke 9.18-24

The Son of Man must undergo great suffering...
If any want to become my followers,
let them deny themselves,
take up their cross daily and follow me.

An old proverb says: "Suffering brings out the best in people." Is the proverb saying the same thing that Jesus says, but in other words? I have the impression that many Christians think so, or perhaps presume so.

I'd like to suggest this morning that there is a real distinction between the two. Suffering is something that happens to all of us. The cross is something we choose. We reach out and pick it up.

In an airport bookstore, I came across the book *Sources of Strength* (New York: Random House, 1977) by former U.S. president Jimmy Carter, and have since put it in the resource room. It's a series of meditations on scripture, more or less reconstructed from adult Sunday School sessions, which he still leads from his home church in Plains, Georgia. In his essay entitled "The Special Message of Jesus," he writes:

> On my bookshelf I have an interesting book that was published in 1978 called *The 100,* by Michael Hart. It is a ranking of the most influential persons in history. I disagree with a lot of Hart's opinions. For instance, he ranks Jesus third, behind Muhammed and Isaac Newton (Buddha, Confucius, and St. Paul come next). Despite this, it is an interesting text, with

some thought-provoking analyses. For example, Hart explains that he ranks Muhammed first because he was the sole founder of Islam, while Jesus and Paul share the responsibility for Christianity. Muhammed was also a great secular leader, while Jesus Christ refused to accept any worldly authority. What is most pertinent is the author's description of the unique message of Christ. Almost all religions adopt some form of the Golden Rule as a premise, but Jesus was alone in commanding that we forgive enemies, turn the other cheek, or walk a second mile. Hart then suggests that if these words and others from the Sermon on the Mount "were more widely followed, I would have no hesitation placing Jesus first in the book." (p. 20)

I think he's onto something. Christianity demands something beyond the "Golden Rule" and beyond the mere endurance of life's hardships. It involves conscious and difficult choices.

The invitation offered to take up the cross is among the most familiar verses in the gospels—and the most challenging. Can it possibly mean simply to accept arthritis, cancer, an unhappy marriage, being expelled from school, or going bankrupt as a "gift" from God, a cross to be borne, making you more like Jesus? Can it involve simply accepting trials and tribulations as they come along, or does the witness of Jesus himself signal "choosing" some suffering on your own? Is grinning and bearing this homily, especially since it's pretty hot in church today, a cross? Maybe! You are making a choice, aren't you? The cross of Christ was chosen. The cross was not for him, nor can it be for us, something accepted passively, or merely endured. It is picked up and embraced.

Jimmy Carter gives an excellent example of this in the person of Clarence Jordan, who had a great influence on Carter's own life. In the 1940s, Jordan founded Koinonia Partners on a farm not far from Carter's home in Plains. It was one of the few places in the Deep South where black and white people could live, work and worship together. To be a part of such a community involved clear choices, and not easy ones. Local merchants boycotted their produce, the Ku Klux Klan attacked and burned crosses from time to time, but the partners persisted, choosing to believe in the potential in all human beings for humanity, mutuality and generosity. Clarence Jordan's farm eventually evolved into the Habitat for Humanity movement with which many of us are familiar even here in Ottawa, and in which Jimmy and Rosalynn Carter are still deeply involved.

To take up the cross is not simply to accept suffering as it comes along, but to embrace an ethical, moral and spiritual standard for life based on the standard Christ chose for himself.

In the language of liturgy and theology, we speak about the sacrifice of Jesus, his gift of self. In the eucharistic prayer we proclaim: "Before he was given up to death, a death he *freely accepted,* he took bread and gave you thanks. He broke the bread, gave it to his disciples, and said: 'Take this, all of you, and eat it: this is my body which will be *given up* for you.'"

Notice how active the verbs are, how conscious, how intentional.

Carter remembers how someone once asked Clarence Jordan if he had participated in the famous freedom rides of the 1960s. He replied: "No, but I've always ridden freely."

To be Christian is to make a free choice to embrace the cross of Christ. The Christian life is a "ride" freely chosen—through the cross to fullness of life.

His Face Set for Jerusalem

Thirteenth Sunday in Ordinary Time

1 Kings 19.16b, 19-21
Psalm 16
Galatians 5.1, 13-18
Luke 9.51-62

"When the days drew near for him to be taken up, Jesus set his face to go to Jerusalem." To be "taken up"? What's that all about? He "set his face." An unusual but interesting expression.

Earlier in Chapter 9, Luke reports that Jesus took Peter, John and James, and went up on the mountain to pray. While there, they saw Moses and Elijah in dazzling splendour talking to Jesus of his departure, which he was about to accomplish in Jerusalem. Here the text suggests that the conversation bore some good results, and hints at its content. Let's focus here on the references to Elijah.

Even though messengers had prepared the way, residents of a certain Samaritan village pay no attention to Jesus. It seems to be his fault. *Face set for Jerusalem*, he was paying no attention to them. James and John, who are with Jesus on the mountain, suggest that they call fire down on them. Jesus rebukes them and they go on.

Do you remember Elijah's experience with calling down fire? It was grand! He and the prophets of Ba'al each prepared wood for a fire. Elijah suggested that they should pray to see if Ba'al would light the fire for them. He would do the same, invoking the God of Israel. The prophets did their thing, singing and dancing. Elijah taunted them, teasing them that Ba'al might be sleeping, or out of town. *No fire*. Then Elijah dug a trench around his woodpile, poured water over it until even the trench was filled with water, offered his prayer and ka-boom!! There was fire! You may remember as well that this "miracle" accomplished nothing except to embarrass the prophets of Ba'al.

Wicked Queen Jezebel was even angrier and determined to be rid of Elijah. He fled to the hills and prayed to die. The text suggests that Elijah's presence on the mountain is a reminder that this stuff just won't do the trick. Nobody's really going to be moved by magic fire, at least not in the right way or for lasting reasons.

Our first reading today presents another parallel. In the gospel someone came up and said, "I will follow you, Lord; but let me first say farewell to those at my home." Jesus said to him, "No one who puts a hand to the plough and looks back is fit for the kingdom of God."

Elijah responds differently to a similar request by his chosen successor, Elisha. He has left his ploughing and accepted the call but first wants to go home to "kiss his father and mother." Elijah agrees. Once at home, Elisha takes leave of his family and his occupation very dramatically. He takes the yoke off the oxen, removes the plough and burns them. He slaughters the oxen and cooks their meat for a farewell feast. Doesn't this have sacrificial overtones?

We could make other references and comparisons between Jesus and Moses and Elijah, but these two very dramatic ones serve the purpose. They give us insight into just why Jesus comes across in such an uncompromising way here. It's as if he learned something from his conversation on the mountain: in his prayer, it became clear to him just how urgent and radical his own mission would be and how correspondingly urgent would be his call to the disciples.

Jesus is not going to be taken up into heaven in a fiery chariot as Elijah was. Moses' presence on the mountain and the allusions to him here may even reflect the tradition that, although he never entered the Promised Land, no one knows where he was buried. Perhaps he too had been taken up in some special way.

Although in this passage, which follows almost immediately, Jesus converses with Moses and Elijah on the mountain, he is expressing both continuity and discontinuity with their stories. Jesus is like and unlike Moses and Elijah. To be a disciple of Jesus will be like, but unlike, anything that has gone before.

Jesus will ascend to God from Jerusalem—by way of the cross. What that will mean for the disciples will be clarified further in Luke's second volume, the Acts of the Apostles. For the moment, the issue is getting to Jerusalem and dealing with the cross. The challenge is "setting your face" in that direction. Discipleship requires, even at this first stage, absolute, unwavering commitment to what Jesus calls the kingdom of God.

Is this fidelity and determination beyond human possibility? It may seem so, and God knows that we all have our stories of lapses, even collapses. Isn't it true, though, however harsh and uncompromising Luke makes it sound, that the persons we have come to admire most are not necessarily the most powerful (who call down fire) or even the most brilliant, or the wittiest, or those who have achieved the highest levels of professional success, but those who have stamina and determination to stay the course, to hold on to their dreams and ideals, even in the midst of apparent failure.

I read recently, for example, how former American president Jimmy Carter is one of the most admired persons not only in the U.S., but in the world. What explains that? Is it like that old comparison between shooting stars and the North Star? One flashes across the sky and is gone before you're even sure it was there, and the other is there night after night "shedding light over the world."

"Thy kingdom come," we pray, and to that kingdom we set our face.

God's Abundant Breasts

Fourteenth Sunday in Ordinary Time

Isaiah 66.10–14
Psalm 66
Galatians 6.14–18
Luke 10.1–12, 17–20

How new can new be? Isaiah has something to say about that.

The exile of Israel in Babylon was interpreted in biblical times as punishment for sin, for social and economic disorder. The Babylonian king and armies were God's instruments of purification. The situation was so bad and the people and their rulers so stubborn that total destruction and a new beginning were the only possibilities left open to God. So far, so good.

After about three generations in exile, the punishment was over. Cyrus the Persian, another divine instrument, conquered Babylon and freed the people of Israel to return to their home, now largely a deserted ruin. Some of them took him up on his offer. They had no personal memory of the "bad old days"—only second- and third-hand information, which may have been passed on by parents and grand-parents. What they *did* have is an invitation to "new days." So far, still so good.

The prophet Isaiah suggests that this once powerful economic and military force suffered God's punishment by humiliation at the hands of her enemies and is now given another chance. This time Israel is destined to be powerful in a new way: God's blessings will not be measured in military or even in economic terms but (are you ready for this?) in "abundant breasts." No kidding!

The new up-and-coming community, the new society, is not likened to a just king and his subjects, a powerful general and his troops, a wise teacher and his students, but to a mother and nursing babies—

an abundant mother at that. The shape of the nation's restoration is likened to the happiness of babies nursing at full breasts, and revelling in maternal caresses.

These metaphorical delights overturn the going expectations about what authority, power and order are all about. It may be because it is so counter-cultural even today that we have shied away from them in preaching and teaching, and have largely lost the maternal side of God's being and God's ways in popular religious imagination. We are more comfortable with kingdom images (not "of this world," we add), surely characterized more by law and order than by nursing and caressing.

When most of us think of God, kings, generals, teachers and even fathers come to mind more immediately than mothers—mothers with breasts full of milk at that. Earlier this morning, one of our male lectors remarked that he felt a bit uncomfortable, even embarrassed, about proclaiming this text.

To overturn popular (and false) interpretations of God's place in the world and the real nature of God's plan, Isaiah chooses to speak of a river of life, an abundant, consoling breast. It's wild! And what is the end or purpose of it all? What is the goal of this newly envisioned community? Not law and order as much as "fresh, new, growing things" ... perhaps better, "fresh, new, growing people"!

I know we may even be a bit uncomfortable with it ourselves, but do we see our church as a "sacrament of God's abundant breasts"? Dear me! But that's the invitation offered to Israel so long ago. Does the image have perennial value? I suggest it does, and so does Luke's gospel.

In our text today, Jesus dispatches a group of disciples, seventy-two of them, which is a traditional symbolic enumeration of all the nations of the world. The disciples are to journey *everywhere*. He himself is *en route* to Jerusalem for the great Passover where the kingdom will be definitively established. "Lambs in the midst of wolves," he is sending them, without "purse, bag or sandals," only a word: "Peace to this house." If the word is not accepted, simply leave the place, he tells them. If it is accepted, stay there. Be there. God is at work where peace is received.

And what are the signs of the kingdom, or perhaps better (paired with Isaiah), what are the signs that "Mother" is at work, or that peace is being received? Healings and exorcisms! Disoriented lives are being reclaimed; broken lives are coming together; self-esteem is being restored; bruised and wounded people are being healed. People are being nurtured, held, hugged and caressed.

The need of persons, families, households and towns for a word of peace is real. In the Bible the greeting of peace is not a wish, but a command: "Peace to this house." Peace is real. It exists. Let it be with you. Be ready to respond to its presence. Know that you can be well with yourself, with your family, with the world and with God! Peace to this house.

To towns and villages, peoples and nations, the messengers of Mother God go with the word: not with social theories, plans for new weapons systems, or even new codes or catechisms, but with a river of life, a consoling breast available to all. As individuals and as a parish, can we find better ways of being instruments, sacraments, incarnations of such a God as this? Can we do a better job, not just in teaching, providing and organizing, but in caressing and fondling—in nursing?

How new can new be? What do you think?

Go and Do Likewise

Fifteenth Sunday in Ordinary Time

Deuteronomy 30.10-14
Psalm 69 or Psalm 19
Colossians 1.15-20
Luke 10.25-37

When he saw him, he was moved with pity. He went to him.... "The word is very near to you, it is in your mouth and in your heart for you to observe."

Throughout the Hebrew Scriptures there is an inseparable connection between the observance of God's law and a peaceful, harmonious life. But how can you observe the law if you don't know the law? Thus, the value of study and ongoing discussion.

One danger in all of this is to reduce the whole matter to externals or "legalism": studying the law to learn its prescriptions and simply "do them," rather than to appreciate or meditate upon real values. We may have been told: "Do it because I said so," not "Do it because it is good and right, and this is why"; or "Don't do this because it is a sin," not "Don't do this because it is destructive or hurtful, and this is how."

This is the context of Moses' speech as well as Jesus' conversation with the lawyer. The context of these texts is just as important as their content. People want to know and understand the law so they can live it and subsequently enjoy God's blessings. How do we do that? Moses and Jesus are both dealing with that issue. Let's explore their approaches further.

Moses says: "Obey the Lord your God by observing his commandments and decrees that are written in the book of the law," but goes on, "Turn to the Lord your God with all your heart and with all your soul." In Luke's gospel, the lawyer, in his conversation with Jesus, adds "and with all your strength, and with all your mind." It's not only about knowing the rules, but about appropriating values in relationship with God, their living source. To study the law is to converse with the Lord, with mind, heart and soul fully engaged in the search for what is right and good. To meditate upon the law is to be in communion with God. What follows is a beautiful expression of God's presence in the depths of our own being. Moses insists that the truth is not in the heavens or across the sea. "The word is very near to you; it is in your mouth and in your heart for you to observe."

In his own way, Jesus is making the same point with the lawyer in the gospel. When the question is posed, "What must I do to inherit eternal life?" Jesus answers with two questions of his own. "What is written in the law?" and "What do you read there?" They sound like the same question, but reflect different emphases; first, what *is* there?— and second, what *do you read* there? What do you see, or get out of it? How you understand or interpret it?

"You shall love the Lord your God with all your heart, and with all your soul, and with all your strength, and with all your mind; and your neighbour as yourself."

"You have given the right answer; do this and you will live."

The law of God does not merely impose an outward submission to certain "do's and don'ts." Rather, it is a principle of life that calls forth an inward response at the very depths of our being. The word comes to life in our reading of it—a living conversation with a living God who animates good moral decisions.

The gospel notes that it is to "justify himself" that the lawyer poses the further question: "And who is my neighbour?" "I can't figure it out for myself," he seems to be saying. "Narrow the field for me … it's too big for me." Recognizing that he's not living the law fully, is he looking for a loophole? It's the kind of question that he could be asking for the rest of his life and never find an answer: a delaying tactic. Such questions are asked not to gain clarity, but to muddy the waters.

"I can't help everybody. Maybe in principle everybody is my neighbour, but in this case do I have to do this or that? Is this really *my* problem? I can't take on the world." A compassionate teacher or counsellor might respond: "Now, now, of course you can't do it all.

Don't drive yourself crazy; do your best." Such taming of the law misses the point.

Jesus does not deal with this question at all, but goes on with the parable of the priest, Levite and Samaritan. Then he poses his final question: "Which of these three do you think was a neighbour to the man who fell into the hands of robbers?" Once again, the lawyer gives the right answer: "The one who showed him mercy." The fact that it is a Samaritan who is the neighbour is particularly impressive. A despised foreigner who is largely ignorant of the law, who may not know the answer, still gets it right.

Ask not who your neighbour is, but meditate with all your heart, soul, mind and strength about what being a neighbour is all about and you will find life.

The "Go and do likewise," which concludes the conversation, points to its deepest layer of meaning. What does the Samaritan do? Yes, he showed him mercy, but first he was "moved with pity." Something happens to him before he does anything, and it is what happens to him that determines his action. "Moved with pity, he showed him mercy."

The passive verb here is very important: "moved with pity." In the original Greek it implies that something is arising out of the depths of one's being that "shakes" the whole person. Have you ever experienced being so moved? It is used elsewhere in the gospel only to describe the love of Jesus or the love of God: for example, Jesus' reaction when he sees the widow of Naim going out to bury her only son, or the father's response when he sees the prodigal son out on the road. To be a neighbour is first of all to be open to enfleshing Jesus' own movement of soul, which in turns enfleshes the love of God.

I found a little morning prayer that I'll read to you. I have no idea who its author is. It invites us to be open to this consciousness.

God, give me the courage of my conviction this day
that you are alive and well in me.
Help me not to waver.
Help me not to procrastinate.
Help me not to rationalize.
Help me not to play games with myself.

Help me to stand strong in Thee.
Help me not just to give what I have,
but to give who you are within me.

The Better Part

Sixteenth Sunday in Ordinary Time

Genesis 18.1–10a
Psalm 15
Colossians 1.24–28
Luke 10.38–42

There are certainly lessons to be learned from how Luke contrasts the figures and personalities of Martha and Mary in today's gospel. It seems that the two most important lessons that Luke would have us take from this story are first, a lesson about relationships, and second, a lesson about our own understanding of who we are.

First, relationships. Have you ever been to a social occasion or a dinner party where those into whose home you have been invited are so preoccupied with the way the place looks and with exactly how the main feature of the dinner is being prepared that the levels of comfort, conversation and ease among the guests are really inhibited? There is so much concern for details that persons are not communing. The whole point of the social engagement, the whole point of the meeting, is compromised because of all the details and all the little things that claim their attention. I once knew a couple who all of a sudden realized that they were together—after their children had grown up and left home. They had been so busy over the years that they scarcely knew each other anymore. They really had a hard time just being together in this new, less stressful situation. They recognized that over all those years they had been busy doing important things, but their own communion hadn't been deepening. It's more important to be in communion with each another even if it's over a hot dog than to fuss over a gourmet feast. Martha seems to have lost sight of the principal values of hospitality and communion.

The second lesson is found in the figure of Mary, who sits at the feet of Jesus in the classical posture of a disciple. In that culture, a woman would never assume that posture. A woman would never be the disciple of a master, responsible and committed to carry on his work after he died. Martha was doing what, in her culture, were the more womanly things. Even in her posture Mary simply transcends that role very dramatically, very radically. What other people think she should be listening to, what other people think she should be doing, what other people think she should be all about, isn't as important as what she really wants for herself. She takes this stance, sitting at the feet of Jesus.

In response Martha is distracted, worried and nervous. Mary is not functioning in an appropriate way. It's more than just "I need her to help me." It's that "Her position, her stance at the feet of Jesus threatens me, bothers me, distracts me. It threatens my own understanding of who I am as I'm busy about all of this stuff in the kitchen."

Jesus says, "Mary has chosen the better part." Mary is communing. Mary is entering into personal relationships. Mary is being who she is. Mary is transcending barriers. Mary is being herself, her deepest and best self. Of course the details are important, but what Mary has chosen for herself cannot be taken from her.

This story brings us face to face with the message of hospitality, of the primacy of human relationships in the busy-ness of life and of the refusal to allow culture or external kinds of things to decide for you who you are going to be and what you will stand for as a person. With typical simplicity, Luke places the personalities of these two women in a very simple setting, and invites us to think deeply about what matters in our relationships with each other and what matters in our sense of our own vocation in life.

Praying as Jesus Prayed

Seventeenth Sunday in Ordinary Time

Genesis 18.20–21, 23–32
Psalm 138
Colossians 2.6–14
Luke 11.1–13

There was once a famous rabbi who was interpreting for his congregation their escape from a certain catastrophe. He told the people it wasn't their fasting or their litanies that made the difference; it was a woman, a poor woman, who had put a little sense into the head of the Almighty. She wept and prayed and cried: "Master of the Universe, are you not our father? Why do you not listen to your children? Look at me, a mother. I have five children, and when they cry, my heart is broken. Look at you—hard-hearted, deaf old thing. Can't you hear your children crying?" She was fighting with God, giving God a little lesson in compassion, which he apparently needed. The rabbi concluded that it was her prayer that saved them. A heavenly decree had been overturned.

Abraham, too, is giving God a lesson, this time in justice and fairness. Abraham's appeal to God recognizes that it's one thing to punish the guilty and quite another to punish the innocent. Justice is being compromised and God's anger is out of control. With rhetorical questioning that is almost whimsical, Abraham asks if the Almighty would not spare the city for the sake of fifty, forty-five, forty—and then starts counting backwards by ten instead of five: thirty, twenty, ten innocent persons. The logic of his movement has no reason for not reducing the number to one, but Abraham lets God figure that out for himself. "Far be it from you," he argues.

After telling a parable about a man banging on his neighbour's door, Jesus calls for similar persistence in prayer, especially when things seem desperate. Central to the parable's interpretation is its context, following, as it does, immediately after the giving of the Lord's Prayer.

The disciples saw Jesus at prayer. Polite enough to wait until he was finished, they asked him to teach them to pray as he was praying. The content of the Lord's Prayer is so familiar that we might miss the significance of Jesus' answer, especially as it is coupled with the parable and Jesus' insistence on dogged determination.

What's involved in praying as Jesus prayed? What is the gospel trying to get across?

First of all, I am to address God in familial terms. God is to be engaged in intimate conversation. God is honoured by being taken so seriously as to be addressed personally. In this way his name is hallowed.

Secondly, there's the primacy of the first petition: "Your kingdom come." It's not about being sure what that means for me personally or for the society and culture of which I am a part, but about asking anyway.

In the meantime there's room to consider my daily bread, the resources I need to live well and creatively today, even if I'm not sure what those are either. Ask anyway.

I am also to acknowledge my sinfulness and to remember how challenging forgiveness and reconciliation are, even in my limited experience.

"And finally, by the way, dear God," I continue, "I'm not looking for any big trouble. I'm not sure just how much I can take, but would rather not be pushed to my limits, thank you very much."

In practice, that kind of prayer will not always sound so solemn, but will inevitably be accompanied at times by bargaining devices, cries, and fist-shaking at the heavens. Precisely because of its real life content does Jesus know that dogged determination will be required. To plead for the conversion and redemption of the world and to be ready to be a part of it, even against great odds, is no small matter.

Far from a wish list, the Lord's Prayer is an act of hope. To pray it is to be fully and positively engaged with God and with life's deepest possibilities. How can God not answer such a prayer, especially when God sees us doing our bit about bread, about reconciliation, and about standing up to tests and temptations of various kinds? "Far be it from you ... not to hear my cries," we are invited to insist.

How God answers is another matter. "If you, then, who are evil, know how to give good gifts to your children, how much more will the heavenly Father give [not good gifts as in Matthew's telling of this story, but the *Holy Spirit*] to those who ask him!"

We would be wrong to think that this is a cop-out. You won't get what you ask, but you'll get the Holy Spirit, spiritual gifts, whatever they are, and whose presence or absence can't be proven anyway. It is not even enough to say that the gift of the Spirit is the supreme grace that surpasses or contains all good things.

We need to read the rest of the gospel and to look into Luke's second volume, the Acts of the Apostles, for a full understanding of what this Holy Spirit is all about. It is wind and fire, the active principle of energy and community life. It inspires commitment, decisions and courage to carry them out.

Luke saw that Jesus' own prayer to God was answered by the gift of the Spirit, and that the same Spirit is God's gift to believers.

Luke is suggesting that to pray is to hope: to search, to knock, to engage the living God and to be ready for the fact that your prayers might just be answered in ways beyond your wildest imagination. The Holy Spirit is yours for the asking.

Henri Nouwen has a typically powerful yet gentle way of bringing these elements together:

Hope means to keep living
amid desperation
and to keep humming
in the darkness.
As long as there is still hope
There will also be prayer.
And God will be holding you close....

With Open Hands
(Notre Dame: Ave Maria Press, 1972), page 85.

Vanity of Vanities

Eighteenth Sunday in Ordinary Time

Ecclesiastes 1.2; 2.21-23
Psalm 90
Colossians 3.1-5, 9-11
Luke 12.13-21

"What do mortals gain from a life of toil and strain?" is the subtitle the lectionary gives to today's text from Ecclesiastes, and what a text it is! "Vanity of vanities," says the Teacher, "vanity of vanities, all is vanity."

"Vanity of vanities" is a Hebraic form of superlative, like saying "biggest" instead of plain old "big." We are left to wonder what this teacher's own life experience must have been for him to be so convinced that all things are "utter emptiness." His further observations address a familiar situation: an ambitious, hardworking person devotes his life's time, toil and worry to practical, down-to-earth affairs, only to die and leave the substantial property that he has accumulated to an heir who has done nothing to deserve it or contribute to it.

In Jesus' story of the rich man and his barns, the teacher's rhetorical generalities come alive. The story could as easily have come from the morning paper as from the gospel. Capital resources, personal wealth or good insurance, as important as these are for prudent people, are no guarantee against heart attack, Alzheimer's disease, or a traffic accident ... but are they sheer vanity? "Vanity of vanities"—or, as the gospel puts it, "You fool!"

It's noteworthy that in these texts the word "vanity" or "emptiness," not evil, is used of such pursuits, and God rebukes the man in the gospel about foolishness, not wickedness.

The inevitability of death plays an obvious role here. "You can't take it with you." When I was reading about funeral rites, I learned that in some parts of Africa, people are completely undressed before they are buried. They go out as they came in. All gain, all merit, all growth in between birth and death must have happened between the walls of your skin, or it has not been real. You can take nothing into the next life but your own person. The meaning in all this seems to be, "What does all this matter? You're going to die one day and you can't take it with you," but beyond the question of death, I wonder if there's not more being said.

This very night your life is being demanded of you.
And the things you have prepared, whose will they be?
So it is with those who store up treasures for themselves
But are not rich towards God.

Is this "life being demanded" just about you on your deathbed? What does it mean to be "rich towards God"?

We had some tragic drowning accidents over the course of the summer. If one of those young people were your son or your granddaughter, what resources would you have?

If your wife were diagnosed with Alzheimer's disease, and you could see her "leaving" you before your eyes, what riches would permit you to cope?

These are not hypothetical cases, because some of our families are dealing with precisely these issues, and all are learning for themselves about being "rich towards God" when life is being demanded.

Let's expand these images even further.

A man who was fussing with his brother over an inheritance got Jesus going with the parable in the first place. What's more important? His relationship with his brother or the money? Vanity of vanities.

Not long ago I was in line at the hardware store behind a young man with a great big cart full of stuff. I overheard his conversation with the checkout lady, with whom he evidently had gone to high school. He had his own business and was working fourteen-hour days during the summer while the weather was good. His wife was working too. They were trying to get ahead. Their two sons, ages seven and nine, would be at camp for most of the summer. I sensed an uneasiness in his voice—that he might be missing something. I know it's none of my business, and that we're not supposed to judge, but "Vanity of vanities"? "You fool"? Strong language, but it does ask us to check in with our values and priorities.

There's been talk of still deeper cuts to art and music education in the schools and more generally to the arts in society. Apparently there are other, more pressing needs in society. What would they be? I always thought that painting and singing and dancing were ways of being "rich towards God."

I was talking with a lady last summer about her son's career choices. He's an all-round bright guy and could do anything he wanted with his life, but had decided to do a basic liberal arts program with a philosophy major. Then he was planning to hitchhike around the world. I don't know how you do that, but according to her that was his plan. She had it in her head that he'd go straight through with a Master's in Business Administration or something equally useful, and was thinking about not contributing financially to his education until he came to his senses. "Vanity of vanities!"

Is all this about evil or wickedness, or is it about short-sightedness or foolishness? Is it about being good and bad, or about being smart and stupid?

Both Ecclesiastes and the parables of Jesus stand in the wisdom tradition. They are not as much about clear moral teaching as they are about discernment of values and true wisdom, about discovering ways to live life fully. Although often expressed in negative terms, they are about getting the most out of life and putting the most back in.

Listen up!

The Middle of the Road

Nineteenth Sunday in Ordinary Time

Wisdom 18.6-9
Psalm 33
Hebrews 11.1-2, 8-19
Luke 12.32-48

Now faith is the assurance of things hoped for, the conviction of things not seen.

Do not be afraid, little flock … Make purses for yourselves that do not wear out … Where your treasure is, there is your heart … Be dressed for action and have your lamps lit.

Have you ever been all dressed up with no place to go? I was talking to a young woman last spring. She had just graduated from university and there was no job out there waiting for her. Issues such as faith, conviction and fear were very real for her, as were values, purses and treasure. Today's scriptures are for her: they encourage faith and steadfastness. It's neat, isn't it, to see once in a while how pertinent the scriptures can be, especially for someone else. I guess that's especially true for someone like me whose job it is to help others make these connections.

Sometimes it is amazing how immediately scripture speaks to a person's life and provides a clear sense of direction. I know people, however, who believe that this is what scripture is for and how it's supposed to work. Some people even close their eyes, open the Bible, point to a verse, open their eyes, and look where their finger is pointing for an answer to the "problem of the day." Eventually, they discover for themselves that this just doesn't work, and that this is not how God's living word operates.

The scriptures offer, not immediate answers, but invitations to question more deeply in pursuit of answers that will hold. In the scriptures, God is asking to be part of the conversation, which may get feisty and rowdy at times, as we try to let many voices be heard and come to peace in a point of view or sense of direction. In traditional language, it's called "discernment," although I find the word a bit quieter and more "interior" than the process turns out to be, at least in my experience of it.

The Jewish sage Ben Hei Hei describes a similar conversational movement:

> We are here to do,
> and through doing to learn,
> and through learning to know,
> and through knowing to experience wonder,
> and through wonder to attain wisdom,
> and through wisdom to find simplicity,
> and through simplicity to give attention,
> and through attention to see what needs to be done.

> from *Wisdom of the Jewish Sages* by Rabbi Rami M. Shapiro,
> quoted in Frederic and Mary Ann Brussat, *Spiritual Literacy*,
> (New York: Scribner, 1996), page 353.

There sure is more going on here than just putting your finger in the Bible, isn't there!

Such discernment is applied in matters great and small, dealing with both personal and social concerns. It isn't trial and error, but there is a certain experiential quality to it. Nobody can tell you the answer. You have to discover it.

Let's try a couple of "for instances."

• Because everybody does it, it is probably interesting and fun.

• Because everybody does it, it is probably common, plebeian, bourgeois and boring.

Where do you stand on that one? For most things, most of us would find ourselves leaning one way or the other.

Going deeper, let's take the issue of family values, so often at the forefront of moral, social and even political discussions. They're usually expressed in terms of marriage, and then in terms of father, mother and children under one roof assuming more or less traditional roles, traditional at least in terms of 1950. Are these values normative for the future, or are they not? Some would say that they reflect the will of God. Others would say that they are not only unrealistic, but degrading for women, demeaning for gays, the artificial creation of a patriarchal, homophobic element in religion and society that refuses to give up its presumed authority and power. Tough talk, eh? We've all heard it. Does the truth lie somewhere in between? *In media stat virtus,* goes the old maxim. Virtue is in the middle of the road. Can that be?

In the spirit of Luke's gospel, I'd like to suggest today that the truth *lies* nowhere, but is discovered in its quest. It lies nowhere, but can be discovered in the middle of the road as you walk along with Jesus to Jerusalem.

Even though I hate the word "comfortable," I think Luke is saying that to be comfortable with being on the road all the time is already to possess the treasure. This is the great nobility in the faith of Abraham and Sarah, in the courage of Israel and in the alertness of parable purse makers, treasure seekers, persons dressed and ready for a party and prudent managers. We are invited to join them, to meet them, each other and the Lord as we move forward with intelligence, humility and grace.

To Be a Principled Person

Twentieth Sunday in Ordinary Time

Jeremiah 38.1–2ab, 4–6, 8–10
Psalm 40
Hebrews 12.1–4
Luke 12.49–53

Jesus makes a strong, dire prediction about tension and division even within the intimacy of our own home. His are harsh, strong words, presenting frightening possibilities, as does the text from Jeremiah, which sounds like something that could happen in a place like Haiti today, where the generals render the president powerless and do what they please with anyone who would oppose their particular way. People *are* put in mud holes today to try to silence them. It's not that going into a mud hole is a value. It's not that creating tension in the family is a value. It's rather that any person who has strong convictions, strong personal values, anyone who stands for anything at all, needs to be ready for a struggle, possibly even within their own home.

Many of us heard the story of St. Francis of Assisi as children. During the Middle Ages, Francis of Assisi's father was a very prosperous man, a merchant of fine cloth. Francis, who worked with him and dressed as a part of that social group, chose to throw off everything that was associated with his family's social rank. In the highly romanticized movie *Brother Sun, Sister Moon*, Francis stands in the public square, throws off his finery and clothes himself in a brown sack as a sign of the new life that he was undertaking. Eventually the sack was refined and stylized into the Franciscan habit that we still recognize today. Francis didn't make this gesture to divide his family, but for the value at stake. In my own family, I think about my grandfather's aunt who left home at sixteen to join the Sisters of St. Joseph in Salina, Kansas; I know the stories of her struggle about that choice and her

162

parents' disapproval of her decision, which she made more than a hundred years ago. In my own generation, a friend was in the seminary. He left the seminary, but was fascinated with philosophy and theology and wanted to continue his education in that field. His parents said, "You are going to finish, David. You are going to finish and you are going to have two choices: washing dishes or driving a taxi. What are you going to do with a Master's in philosophy?" What would they have said in today's economy, which is even more challenging on these topics? How do people discover core values and move with them?

There are Jeremiahs around, too: victims of death squads in places like El Salvador; someone bottled up in a hole somewhere in China for dissenting. Even within the history of the church there have been people who have been isolated and silenced for a while. Sometimes it's only long afterwards that the real value of their contribution is recognized. We are still silencing people and jailing them because they stand for something that threatens society, because their heart and head are leading them in a different direction, in ways that create tension, sometimes within the intimacy of their own families. Jesus says, "If that happens, it's worth it. You can't allow pressure of any kind to compromise your deepest personal self."

The radical language of both the Jeremiah story and Christ's teaching in today's gospel does apply to our life experience. How often do we hear about baby boomers, for example? Marketing people target baby boomers. Politicians target baby boomers to get their support. What does that mean? Are baby boomers all alike? Look back over your own personal history: what was it like in the 50s? The 50s had a spirit. The 60s, the 70s, the 80s—each decade was characterized by its own philosophical, economic and spiritual way of being and thinking. To be a religious person, to have faith, to have Christian values, makes us critical of trends and movements. To be caught up in such trends without realizing it is a serious problem. To think, to stand for something, to be a principled person is really the challenge presented by Jeremiah, who was so utterly principled that he found himself in a mud hole. It's the challenge of Jesus himself who is so utterly principled that he finds himself on the cross.

Of course, we need to grow and change, and to have within ourselves a kind of flexibility. But to stand for nothing except what is

163

going on is really to "lose your soul." That's what Jesus means when he uses that language in his teaching: he invites us to be, not stubborn ideologues, but principled persons who live, decide and critique the society of our own generation. Christianity, like any real religious faith, demands that critique. Christ's teaching in today's gospel puts that challenge in the most dramatic, radical, strident way possible. We need to recognize, that stridency notwithstanding, that his challenge applies to us in our own culture today.

The Narrow Door

Twenty-first Sunday in Ordinary Time

Isaiah 66.18–21
Psalm 117
Hebrews 12.5–7, 11–13
Luke 13.22–30

"Will only a few be saved?" someone asked. Jesus replied: "Strive to enter the narrow door; for many, I tell you, will try to enter and not be able."

We've probably all heard preachers, television evangelists, even some among our own, who need just a pair of verses such as these to be off and running. A question was posed, an answer given: let's go.

"To get in, you have to believe this and only this, not all that other stuff which waters down the truth. Truth is truth; believe and be saved."

"To get in, you have to be clean and pure, have nothing to do with the filth and perversion of the world" (usually referring to sexuality).

"You see, there are a lot more sinners out there than you think. You've all probably got a mortal sin or two on your soul—better get to confession."

The narrow door seems to suggest clear limitations to thinking and restrictions to acting. It seems to imply a certain perfection, completeness, full obedience. A single sin could exclude you from God's house, as will more general evils such as "riches or the cares of this world." Even questioning authority or tradition could be risky. Who, indeed, can be saved?

Once again, Luke just won't let us get away with that sort of clarity. He dismisses such approaches out of hand. He does not directly answer questions such as "Will only a few be saved?" Instead he tells a story.

In the story, those who know the owner of the house, even those who know its floor plan because they "ate and drank with him," are excluded.

"I don't know where you've come from," he replies to their knocking at the door. "I do not know where you've come from; go away from me, all you evildoers."

The parable avoids abstractions such as perfection, truth or worthiness, but deals instead with authenticity, earnestness and integrity. "Where are you coming from?" is a question we ask of someone when we're not quite sure about that person's attitude or approach to an issue. It is a process question.

It's much easier to think in terms of requirements than to engage a person. It's easier to announce "These are the requirements" than to ask, "Where are you coming from?"

People like myself and others involved in pastoral ministry can be tempted to deal with other people at the level of requirements, especially in areas such as the sacraments, where we think we have a certain control. Unless you do this or that, attend this or that meeting, come to church this or that many times, you can't get married here, be confirmed, or have your baby baptized. Fit into the mold, or else. These are the requirements. This is the size and shape of our door! If you can squeeze through it, fine. If not, goodbye and good luck: you're out.

Such an approach is contrary both to the spirit of Jesus and to the canons of the church. The *Code of Canon Law,* by the way, presents universal norms for the sacraments, which are far less restrictive and more hospitable in their approach than those imposed by many Catholic parishes. I shouldn't be passing judgment or even commenting about what goes on beyond my own sphere of influence and responsibility, but I can't help it, because people come here with stories that annoy me very much. Such impositions are contrary to the gospel, contrary to the law of the church—and they won't work anyway.

Some of you, by the way, may want to consider joining a sacramental team. We'll be going over the universal norms, and the approaches to them proposed in our diocese, when our sacramental preparation teams get together in the fall. Throughout the year all of us will want to be hospitable towards strangers who will be coming to this house with their children—however tentatively. We do not always know "where they are coming from," and need the discipline and asceticism to make space for them to be at home enough to share that with us.

The question "Where are you coming from?" poses a number of sub-questions such as: Are you on a road? Do you know what road you're on and why you're on it? In other words, are you living in a dynamic and authentic way? Is your journeying real? Is there sincerity and truth in that journeying?

Luke consistently suggests that those of us who are "saved" and secure in our knowledge of what that is all about may not even be dealing with these essential issues ourselves. We may be either standing still or coming from the wrong place. We could be looking at the door from the wrong angle, or taking its measurements with the wrong ruler.

The sense that many will come from the east and the west, and that the last will be first and the first last, turns upside down any tendency in organized religion to deify the size and shape of any particular door. The issue in hospitality for us who are at home here is less the size and shape of our door than inquiring about where our neighbours are coming from, and washing their feet and anointing their heads.

A prayer is posted on the doors of this church, through which most of us come and go regularly. We borrowed it from St. Stephen's Church, London, England, and posted it to honour the jubilee year. In light of Jesus' teaching about the narrow door, read it carefully as you leave the church today. It's not a requirement prayer, but a process prayer:

> God, make the door of this house wide enough
>   to receive all who need human love and fellowship,
> narrow enough to shut out all envy, pride, and strife.
> Make its threshold smooth enough
>   to be no stumbling block to children,
> nor to straying feet, but rugged and strong enough

to turn back the tempter's power.
God, make the door of this house the gateway
to Thine eternal kingdom.

Gathered at the Table of Life

Twenty-second Sunday in Ordinary Time

Sirach 3.17-20, 28-29
Psalm 68
Hebrews 12.18-19, 22-24a
Luke 14.1, 7-14

"Let each man sit according to his rank. Let the priest sit in the first place, and the elders in the second, and then the rest of the people, let them sit according to their ranks." This statement comes from Qumran, a monastic community near the shore of the Dead Sea. This particular rule, which describes how community meals were organized, reflects how their whole life was organized. There was a clear hierarchy: priests, elders and the rest.

Something in our more egalitarian mindset resists such classes and classifications. In the population at large, there are no formally designated classes such as those at Qumran—priests, elders and the rest, or in ancient Israel—priest, Levites and Israelites. Neither are there commoners and nobles. That's not to say, however, that there are no classes. We have a hard time resisting classifying ourselves.

I was riding the train from Montreal to New York, which is one of my favourite things to do. It's a beautiful trip along the western shore of Lake Champlain and then down the Hudson River. Sitting in the lounge car, I was talking with a very charming lady who was going to a convention of the D.A.R., the Daughters of the American Revolution. I forget all the details, but her ancestors were in one of the colonies before the Revolution. In her mind, she was clearly more American than anyone else she could imagine. Even here in Ottawa, isn't it true that many, even unconsciously, consider themselves "more Canadian" than the new Canadians who became citizens on Canada Day this past July?

As far as meals go, I've been to lots of wedding and other banquets where head tables are organized. Tables for the rest of us are organized as well, sometimes even to the extent of preparing individual place cards. Nothing wrong with that, is there? It can actually be helpful in making people feel welcome and comfortable. As a parish priest, I for one, hardly an extrovert, have often been invited to wedding and anniversary banquets. I'm not always sure where and with whom those who invited me expect me to sit. Trying to figure it out or guess makes me uneasy. Once someone tells me where to sit, I'm fine.

Do you think the gospel today is about that sort of thing? There will always be special groups, even exclusive groups, which will hold special events with head tables and the works. There will always be ladies' bridge clubs, youth groups, Kiwanis Clubs, Richelieu Clubs that will hold banquets and organize tables. What's wrong with that? And about the banquet in the scene that opens the gospel: if the host and those assisting him had been more hospitable in the first place, that embarrassing episode wouldn't have happened at all. Is the moral of the story really about humbly hanging out at the back of the hall on such occasions, so that the host can escort you to an exalted place for all to see? That's silly.

Jesus' comments about the high and low places at table, which reflect certain perennial conventions and rules of etiquette, are really a lead-in to a consideration of table fellowship in broader, more spiritual terms.

Let's take a look at what meals are all about for the ancient world, and especially in Jesus' own understanding of table fellowship.

Consider for a moment how there is nothing that "puts you in your place" more than sitting down to eat. We are not rich or poor, male or female, black or white, French or English when we eat. We are just human—dependent with all other humans on the fruit of the earth for nourishment and life. Even the family cat and the critters she hunts have that in common with us. We are fundamentally dependent upon the earth. Such consciousness stimulates humility and solidarity with all of humanity and with all living creatures gathered at the "table of life."

The grace that many Protestants use at their family tables reflects this consciousness more clearly than the grace with which most of us are more familiar. I may not have the wording exactly right, but it goes something like this: "Bless, O Lord, this food to our use, and us to thy service, and keep us ever mindful of the needs of others."

To eat is to be in communion with all that is. The challenge comes in realizing that truth and living out its consequences in real and practical ways.

Consciousness of what we are doing when we sit down together at a meal encourages humility, solidarity and openness to those with whom we eat, and with the whole of creation. Any distinction of class, or consideration of formalities and rules of etiquette, is clearly of secondary importance in this table spirituality. That Jesus, contrary to the conventions of his time, shared table fellowship with outsiders, even sinners, reflects his awareness of this spirituality, which for him is a high priority in his teaching and in his whole way of being in the world.

Another aspect of table fellowship in the ancient world is that of "wisdom sharing." The table is the most common setting for discussion in the Hellenistic as well as in the Jewish worlds. The Symposium in ancient Greece, for example, is a table around which table-talk is happening: sometimes serious, sometimes frivolous—always of human interest. The meal provides the occasion and the context for "round table discussion." The sharing of food creates an environment for the sharing of wisdom.

For Jesus, these questions emerge: How big is your table? How round? With whom are you ready to talk? Who has wisdom in which you would be interested? Is there room at your table for unlikely sources of life and wisdom: the poor, the crippled, the lame, even "sinners"? With whom do you picture yourself sharing the eternal feast of God's kingdom?

For Jesus, real humility is found in living the meal: living in respect, collaboration and solidarity with all people, with all living things, with all the earth.

Real humility is found in being open and ready to share with and to learn from all people, especially those who seem least likely to have something to teach us.

In that humility persons discover their greatest dignity and potential. In that humility they are exalted.

171

In that humility we approach this table for a foretaste of the eternal feast to come.

When the Cross
Is All That Counts

Twenty-third Sunday in Ordinary Time

Wisdom 9.13-18
Psalm 90
Philemon 9b-10, 12-17
Luke 14.25-33

A weekly faith-sharing meeting takes place here every Thursday after the morning Mass. You may wish to drop in once in a while or even join the group. The group centres its reflection and prayer on the scriptures to be read the following Sunday. One of the people participating mentioned to me on Friday that today's reading is her absolutely least favourite reading in the whole gospel (so far). The group had been puzzling over many of Luke's surprises, but this one was more than she could handle. A strong family person, she feels deeply devoted to her family and even when she doesn't feel like it, she said, her marriage vows commit her to making them her priority. Besides, who wants to be a fanatic? Isn't such total commitment unworthy of human dignity—isn't that what cults are made of? Wow! I wasn't expecting that, nor was I ready for it on my way from Mass to breakfast, especially on Friday, which is supposed to be my day off.

Luke never tires of throwing us off balance. Do you remember how he depicts Jesus' relationship, even at twelve years of age, with his own family? He was "lost" and in the temple.

When his parents saw him they were astonished; and his mother said to him, "Child, why have you treated us like this? Look, your father and I have been searching for you in great anxiety." He said to them, "Why were you searching for me? Did you not know that I must be in my Father's house?" But

173

they did not understand what he said to them. (Luke 2.48-50)

What is this "hating" all about that we find in the gospel today? Scholars tell us that the original word denotes not animosity towards those who are usually nearest and dearest, but a fixation on the priority of, or one's own authenticity and commitment to, the truth reflected in the cross of Jesus. It suggests that nothing and no one would be able to stand between the disciple and Jesus. It speaks of a personal decision or commitment that is not dependent on the understanding or approval of others, even family. There's something about being a disciple of Jesus that transcends all other commitments and relationships.

Tom Harpur, Anglican priest and journalist, points to the importance of this commitment, even for the credibility of religion itself. He points out further how churches have become so enmeshed in society at large that they have appeared to be the very backbone of capitalism and militarism. Where there are conflicts between faith values and patriotism, faith values too easily cave in. He notes a shadow side to organized Christianity beginning already in the fourth century, when the church established a cozy relationship with Constantine and naïvely believed in the possibility of Christendom—a holy empire. Some theologians even equated the church and its political power with the kingdom of God. What in fact often took place was "pouring holy water over the status quo" in order to be safe and secure, or to get the best for its own privilege and power.

The most recent issue to get a lot of press in this regard is the position of Pius XII during the Second World War. It has been charged that he was not vigorous enough in condemning the Nazi persecution of the Jews and, indeed, was all too ready to deal with Hitler and Mussolini. At the same time other Christian individuals, such as Dietrich Bonhoeffer and Maximilian Kolbe, stood firmly against the atrocities. They died as martyrs. They did not, however, have the Pope's global responsibility. The questions are complex, and the issue remains ambiguous. Even more important than evaluating the past, however, is the issue that faces us today. What is the relationship between faith and culture? How and in what sense do religious values and traditions either bless or critique the order of the day?

This question was raised again when then-President Bush called in Billy Graham to spend the night at the White House in order to give him courage and comfort as he initiated the Gulf War. It's not the first time that militarism has been so blessed: witness the flags and military paraphernalia found in many church buildings. Is or is that not appropriate? The answer is not easy, but the question needs to be asked.

Even in the midst of comfortable church–state complicity over the centuries, the "prophetic edge" in Christianity has always been present.

It is true that the church of the white minority buttressed apartheid in South Africa, but it is also true that religious figures such as Desmond Tutu and countless others who are less known, on both sides of the racial divide, raised their voices in protest. Even President deKlerk admitted being shaken from his long-held position by his Christian faith, facets of which he had tried to suppress, but which kept haunting him.

Coalitions and networks of various faith traditions today stand up and try to raise our consciousness about justice issues. Perhaps not very powerful, they are nevertheless very present, and often a thorn in the side of hierarchies—even religious ones. Such groups and movements are clearly on side with Luke's vision of things.

Nothing in Luke's gospel of reversals suggests "I'm okay, you're okay," or that Canada is the best country in the world, so shut up and enjoy it, or that this theological question has already been answered, so stop thinking about it.

Luke follows the hard saying about "hating" and carrying the cross with descriptions of tower building and war waging, which will apparently need well-laid plans and abundant resources. Paradoxically the last verse in the text reads, "So, therefore, none of you can be my disciple if you do not give up all your possessions." How does that follow?

It's clearly not an ordinary tower or an ordinary war to which the text refers. There is a selflessness required in these projects, which are better served by the Desmond Tutus, Mahatma Gandhis and Martin Luther Kings of this world. (Or even Pius XII: It was in mockery of his position that Stalin asked, "How many legions has the Pope?")

Those who have taken Luke's tough sayings of Jesus to heart over the centuries have been a great blessing for the church and for the world. They have kept humanity mindful of what goes beyond the "reasoning of mortals, human designs, and earthly tents" as the Book of Wisdom describes the issues of the day.

For thoughtful and conscientious Christians, there will always be a tension between the political, economic and religious status quo and genuine spirituality. True believers face and live that tension.

Keeping the Lights On

Twenty-fourth Sunday in Ordinary Time

Exodus 32.7-11, 13-14
Psalm 51
1 Timothy 1.12-17
Luke 15.1-32

When little children are getting ready for their first confession, their parents gather to reflect on the role of sin and reconciliation, confession and the sacraments in their own life and in their own experience so that they can communicate with their children about the values involved. A wonderful little film is widely used in preparation programs for the sacrament of penance. The film is a modern adaptation of this prodigal son story. A very traditional, conservative, suburban family lives in a white house with little brass coach lights at the entrances and a porch with columns. Their son is stifled in that environment. Once he gets to be twenty-one, he simply has to get out of there. He explodes; after a lot of unpleasant talk and fuss, the son simply disappears. The film lets us see his pilgrimage as his separation from that very traditional place unfolds: alcohol, drugs and all kinds of other experiences. Finally, he reaches bottom and decides that he should go home. He's lonesome. He's homesick. He's alone. He's confused. He's bewildered. He's still very anxious about his relationship with his parents. He knows he can't just go back. But he gets himself together and writes them a little note saying that he's going to try to get back, and he would understand if they weren't prepared to receive him or talk to him. But, if they're prepared to see him, would they leave the light on at the front door? As he's hitchhiking home, a very nice man picks him up, and they talk about life and growth and change. The driver decides that he won't just go drop him off outside the village; instead he'll go by the house to see if the light is on.

177

He comes by the house. Not only is the front door light on, *all* the lights are on. The house looks like a Christmas tree shimmering in the darkness. Viewers tend to have tears in their eyes at that particular point. And that's where the film ends. You need to imagine what might happen as that story continues to unfold, the dying and rising that would take place in the young man's parents as they try to deal with him now, and with their own expectations, their own sadness, their own alienation, their frustration, their sense of failure. Likewise, it would seem that a dying and rising has to take place in that young man. He has to deal with his pride, his folly, his independence, whatever he has to get together; they all have to deal with each other in a new way. Nothing will ever be the way it was. But the lights are on, providing the invitation that can start things anew.

Think of the story of the prodigal son, and the dying and rising that take place in the father and the younger son, as well as the elder son. He seems to be living at home and fulfilling his duties more out of loyalty, responsibility and obligation than real love or joy. "I've been slaving for you all these years," he says. What's his relationship with his father? It's not too good either, is it? The lights being on; it's hard to keep your lights on. It's not easy to relate to your parents, your grandparents or your children in good times or in bad times. It's not easy to keep the lights on, but it's a very important and essential way of being human. The other alternative, to turn the lights off and close the door, is utterly uninteresting and destructive.

The text from the book of Exodus is almost funny. We can only talk about God as a person by relating him to our own experience. Here is this image of God who is so angry. He's really mad at the people for worshipping the calf, among other things. Moses pokes at God, trying to get God to soften up a little bit. Essentially God says, "Leave me alone. I want to sit here. I'm enjoying my anger. I want to sit here and let my wrath burn. Then I'm going to punish these people; I'll feel a whole lot better. Don't tell me that their ancestors were beautiful people. Don't tell me anything. I don't want to hear any of that. I want to sit here with my wrath and I'm going to enjoy punishing them." It's a funny picture of God, but it so resembles us when we get in a mood. Moses pokes and pokes and pokes, and finally God changes his mind. If God can change his mind, maybe we can

178

too. If God can be flexible, maybe we can too. We need to keep our lights on.

Earlier this week I had a very difficult experience. The man of the household I was visiting started talking about "the French" and the referendum and saying completely outlandish things. The more he talked, the more uncomfortable I became. I guess he could see that I was trying to disappear. Finally, he said, "I guess I'm a little bit carried away." I agreed. Then he told me his story. He works in a situation where bilingualism would be a real asset. Because he's not bilingual, he's been passed over a couple of times. It's very difficult for him to keep the lights on.

Another example this week was just the opposite. I used to be parish priest in Fallowfield. The Houlihan family has been there forever, very Irish, staunchly rural. Peter married a woman, Nicole, from St. Pierre, a little town near Quebec City. The family had four daughters. The father had a stroke when he was quite young and was disabled for years. The mother had a little subsistence job in the Château Frontenac and managed to keep that family together, a beautiful family that had strong roots and solid values. Peter doesn't speak a word of French and none of his wife's family speak English, except Nicole. They had a little joke that if she died first, they would be buried in St. Pierre. If he died first, they'd be buried in Fallowfield.

Nicole and Peter married, but they couldn't have any children. They had a hairstyling business on Bank Street and as soon as they got on their feet financially, they bought a piece of land in St. Pierre. There they built a bungalow for Nicole's parents so they would be a little bit more comfortable.

This week Nicole died of a massive cerebral hemorrhage right at their business on Bank Street. Here they all were at the funeral home. They invited me to go because their pastor can't handle French, and I can handle it a little bit. It was a real privilege. The respect in that place and what Peter had to say about Nicole's family and his experience with them was really touching and beautiful. The language barrier was still there, but the lights were on. In a situation where real people deal with real people in an atmosphere of genuine respect, lights come on in a different way.

At so many different levels of life it's all too easy for us to be like God is in that text from Exodus: almost enjoying being mad at our kids, mad at our parents, mad at the French—mad at something, to enjoy being stuck there.

The text from the gospel acclamation is very beautiful: "God was in Christ," it says. "God was present in Christ to reconcile us to himself." Well, if God can cope with the likes of me, maybe I can cope with the likes of others. The next line is "the good news of reconciliation"—the good news of the wonderful possibilities of reconciliation—"he has entrusted to us." If we're Christian, if we're involved in Christ, if we're saying "Amen" to his body broken for our forgiveness and for our peace, if we gather for holy communion, we recognize that we have been entrusted with that kind of ministry and approach to life. We're invited time and time again, most symbolically and most profoundly at the eucharist, to make sure that the lights are on.

Not "The Same Old Thing"

Twenty-fifth Sunday in Ordinary Time

Amos 8.4-7
Psalm 113
1 Timothy 2.1-7
Luke 16.1-13

Typical of what we've seen so often in Luke's gospel, this parable really turns us around. Hardly edifying, hardly pious, it raises up a thief, a scoundrel, a dishonest manager who is strangely commended. For our purposes today, let's look at the rather straight, usual interpretation of this typical Lucan reversal.

There are people who are prepared to do all kinds of creative, interesting, shrewd, cunning, imaginative things for profit or personal gain. Those who stand for less material values, who may even claim to serve God, may not be so energetic, creative or ready to take risks in pursuit of their goals. In Jesus' words, "The children of this age are more shrewd in dealing with their own generation than are the children of light."

An example of this came up just yesterday. Members of our pastoral council participated in a diocesan meeting on plans for youth ministry. We learned how, for example, MuchMusic, the MuchMusic Channel and many of its videos are commercially driven. They are designed to set a standard about how young people should wear their hair, what kind of jewellery they should wear, where their bodies should be pierced, and what brand names they should go for in their clothing. Apparently they do this with considerable success. This being said, might the church try more creative ways of reaching out to young people to call them beyond certain styles and standards to "fullness of life in Christ"? How ready would our own parish be to risk investing more of our resources into youth ministry, or reducing the number of Sunday morning Masses in favour of an evening celebration which would be more attractive to youth? It's one thing for an organization such as ours to be in favour of something like youth involvement, and quite another to "jump in."

A gentleman stopped after Mass a few weeks ago to chat about what I had said in the homily and promised to get back to me. He wrote me a letter in which he enclosed a copy of an advertisement published in a paper like the *Ottawa Citizen* inviting what we would typically have called "fallen-away Catholics" to take another look at the church. It was a very pro-active invitation for alienated, perhaps even bitter and angry people, to consider "coming home" for Christmas. He was suggesting that our parish, which puts hospitality at the head of its mission statement, might want to take up such a project. We will want to consider it, and if we go ahead, I hope that he'll be part of the team. It's one thing to think about things, quite another to do them.

I recently heard part of a radio interview Peter Gzowski did with a woman in Michigan. (I wasn't able to listen to the whole program because I was *en route* somewhere in my car.) She had been a participant in a twenty-year study on early childhood development in families and communities at risk. The study targeted inner-city families with very young children, and made certain simple opportunities available to them in daycare settings. More staff, some even summer volunteers, who talked to the children, even the infants, who played with them, played classical music for them. I'm sure you can guess what the study showed, leading to the claim that every dollar spent at this initial stage of a child's life will save seven dollars later on. The woman went on to critique decreased funding for such programs as universal daycare and Head Start, and increased preoccupation with longer and tougher jail sentences for juvenile offenders. She wondered why all the attention was given to darkness rather than to the potential for brightness.

I think that her wondering is quite in line with the kind of wondering that gets Jesus into the parable-telling mode.

Jesus sees very clearly into the issues and tensions of his own time. The creative invitations in his parables have perennial value and have challenged the Christian community ever since; not only in terms of goal setting, but also of approach and method in meeting those goals.

His parables, perhaps especially in Luke's gospel, invite us to an ongoing critique of our own life and times, of our personal and societal goals, and of the methods with which we reach out to meet those goals.

His method is quite different from that of the prophet Amos who, in today's first reading, simply lashes out in no uncertain terms against the evils and injustices of his day, and reminds the people of God's judgment. Although he gets into that mode from time to time, by and large, Jesus seems to sense that it doesn't go very far with people. It just doesn't work very well and may even be counterproductive. It's too easy just to name problems. Many of us, even today, have experience with preachers who think they're being prophetic by lashing out against abortion, or against divorce, or against violence and drug abuse among young people, or against missing Mass, and have felt ourselves wishing we had some kind of remote to change channels.

By and large, Jesus' approach is more creative and invitational. He prods and pokes at people, tickling their imagination. To "children of the light," he sometimes suggests in a parable that they are not as enlightened as they think they are. At other times he suggests, as he does today, that there is not enough creative energy at work among them in their reading of and responding to the "signs of their own times."

The living Christ is present today as his word is proclaimed. We are invited to ask ourselves what he might be saying to us in this parable today. Is he suggesting to me, to our pastoral council, to all of us, that there may be creative and untapped ways of "dealing with our own generation" that we haven't even thought of yet, much less tried? Is he suggesting that the "same old thing" can never be good enough for "children of light"? That's what I'm hearing. How about you?

St. Brigid's Deli

Twenty-sixth Sunday in Ordinary Time

Amos 6.1a, 4–7
Psalm 146
1 Timothy 6.11–16
Luke 16.19–31

This parable of the rich man and Lazarus could not possibly present sharper contrasts, or more radical reversals!

There's Lazarus, whose name means "God helps," and the rich man who has no name.

There's the rich man dressed in purple, who feasts sumptuously every day while poor Lazarus lies at his gate, covered with sores, being ministered to by dogs.

There's the poor, sick Lazarus, who is carried by angels to be with Abraham, and the rich man who is unceremoniously buried and doomed to Hades.

In a workshop on preaching in which I participated, the leader asked us to work out approaches to preaching this very parable. Many of the participants decided that the moral of the story was that the rich man, though not mean or wicked towards Lazarus, simply didn't notice him lying there right at his gate. Not only should he have noticed him there, but he should have done something to provide for his nourishment and healing. Too often we don't see and don't act.

Our leader listened patiently and then went on to show that this kind of moralizing was simply not enough. It would go nowhere with our congregations except to produce a "Here we go again" reaction. Even if people listen carefully to this message, what response would the preacher expect? Uneasy guilt? Nobody needs more of that, and besides, stirring up guilt isn't gospel anyway! What good news would that be?

Most of us simply do not have the capacity to take in hungry and wounded street people. Their real care and healing is beyond what any of us rich people could provide. Even if we started taking people in, where would it stop? As soon as one "Lazarus" is looked after, another would take his place. Would we not also run the risk of neglecting our primary responsibilities as spouses, parents and friends? What would ever be enough? What's left in all of this for me? Am I not allowed to be comfortable? ... and the whole process rolls on, going absolutely nowhere. It's hopeless ... especially since the parable seems to indicate that the rich and able-bodied will wind up in Hades if there's even one last Lazarus at the gate. "Lazarus paralysis" sets in.

Here in Ottawa, we're very familiar with the wonderful work of the Shepherds of Good Hope. You may remember that it all started with a soup kitchen out of St. Brigid's Parish Hall. I can't resist telling you my own "Lazarus paralysis" story that happened there before that soup kitchen was established.

One year when I was a graduate student at Saint Paul University, I filled in at St. Brigid's over New Year's to give the pastor a break. A man came to the door asking for a handout. In what I thought was my wisdom, I told him that I didn't have any money to give him, but if he'd like to come in and have something to eat, he'd be most welcome. The housekeeper, who was out with her family, had cooked a big turkey and there was lots left over. I put on the coffee pot and made him a New York-style deli sandwich—lots of meat. I even asked whether he preferred white or dark. If I remember correctly, he preferred 7-Up to Pepsi and had his coffee with pie—also home-made—later.

I'll bet you can already guess what happened the next day. The word hit the streets. St. Brigid's Deli was on the map. But there was no way that its staff of one, even with a fridge full of soft drinks and a leftover turkey, could cope with the demand. More than one Lazarus was neither fed nor healed that day ... at least by my hand.

To get back to that workshop on preaching the Lazarus story: our leader reminded us of the complexities of the world beyond our gate, of media coverage of disaster after disaster, of mailings coming into our homes from countless charitable organizations, of mailing lists of names of generous people sold and traded, of complex, even overwhelming need everywhere, not to mention the deeply rooted social and economic imbalances in our global village. There is a Lazarus everywhere we turn, crying out, tempting us to wish we were deaf.

While the parable reflects the insensitivity and numbness that can set in when people are bombarded by the plight of the less fortunate, other, deeper elements of the parable wait to be uncovered. For example: Isn't there a temptation that we might think that we have earned, deserve and are meant to enjoy our well-being and security? Are we sufficiently aware of the complex social and economic factors that have gone into making us who we are? Is it not also easy to assume that material wealth and well-being can be taken, without qualification or further examination, as a blessing—even from God?

Is it not also true that there's a temptation to think that the poor are so because of their own fault—that they are getting what they deserve? We may not express it that baldly, but is it not part of the undercurrent around perceptions of welfare recipients as lazy and largely responsible for their situation? Is it not also true that the world flatters the rich and powerful, that even the church can be tempted to do so for its own purposes?

As Luke's gospel presents the teaching of Jesus, it's hard to avoid the conclusion that from God's point of view the situation is very different from the one I have been describing. In the person of Lazarus, God vindicates the poor, the oppressed, the excluded of human society without reference to any special virtue or worthiness factor. The only thing that is said about Lazarus is that he was desperate, not that he was virtuous. The only thing said about the rich man is that he is rich, very rich, not that he is evil; he may even have had a favourite charity, but it was elsewhere.

Only after finding the courage to look at the parable more deeply can we begin to hear its good news. As we delve into the parable and struggle with its content, the good news begins to emerge. We gradually discover that the fact that Jesus tells parables like this at all is itself good news. What do I mean by that? Well…

•   It is good news that God has such confidence in us, that God trusts us to be able to deal creatively with life's most profound complexities.

•   It is good news that God believes in us and in our capacity to respond to his call for justice in mature and life-affirming ways.

• It is good news that Jesus does not insult us with clichés or simple answers, that God trusts our human potential to be critical of quick and easy answers, and to be fully engaged in both analysis and response to the fact of "Lazarus."

• It is good news that God thinks we're tough enough to be challenged so deeply, and to have our ordinary ways of thinking critiqued so drastically.

Jesus would not have preached this parable in the first place if he didn't have confidence that we would be able to hear it with generous and creative hearts. He wouldn't have thrown this zinger our way at all if he didn't think we could handle it!

The Flying Tree
and the Slave

Twenty-seventh Sunday in Ordinary Time

Habakkuk 1.2-3; 2.2-4
Psalm 95
2 Timothy 1.6-8, 13-14
Luke 17.5-10

Those of us who garden around here fight a particularly nasty weed. Not only does it seem to grow everywhere, but when you pull it out, it pays you back by giving you a prickly rash on any part of your skin with which it comes into contact. Wouldn't it be fun to "turn up your faith" and send those little devils flying to the sea? Surely if it works with mulberry trees, it would work with those weeds. Oops! Luke is talking about transplanting the mulberry tree into the sea where he suggests it will flourish. I don't think the kids would like this new "seaweed" on their favourite beach, so we might better redirect our "turned up" faith to something else.

It doesn't take much analysis to figure out that Jesus is talking about a different kind of uprooting and transplanting from that which happens with weeds and trees ... but what?

Paired with the mulberry tree is the awkward and uncomfortable parable about "worthless slaves" simply fulfilling their duties because they have no other choice, and suggesting that the human condition is like that. No gratitude expected, no "brownie points," no "moving up the ladder," just work.

Scholars suggest that these two sayings of Jesus were probably not linked originally. Because they have such different emphases, they likely derive from separate occasions in Jesus' preaching ministry. Let's see, though, if we can't make some connections anyway. Can we link in these two images: the wonder of having faith, and the wonder of being faithful?

The apostles begin by asking: "Increase our faith." Have you ever wished for more faith, or asked for more faith yourself? How do you think anybody, even Jesus, could give you more faith? Jesus responds that even with a tiny bit of faith, big things are going to be happening: trees flying, uprooting, re-rooting. Is he saying that, even if we think our faith is not up to the challenge, there will be no impossible task coming our way, no hand of cards dealt that is simply unplayable? "Be positive and confident about the faith you have. Face the day with courage."

Was it Anne of Green Gables who said, "Isn't it a splendid thing that there are mornings?"

In her book *Seasons of Your Heart*, Benedictine Sister Macrina Wiederkehr talks to the morning. She speaks to her as if she were a living person, slipping through the darkness on tiptoe, offering fresh, new and untried possibilities.

Don't hurry, morning;
come slowly.
Dress yourself in light.
Climb over that hill lovingly
Hand me a new day hopefully
Get into my bloodstream, and
colour me like the rising sun
slowly
I've a mind to be contagious
Colour me bright.

Seasons of Your Heart
(New York: Harper Collins, 1991), page 65.

What a wonderful way to welcome a new day! Faithful to the presence of God in our lives, why shouldn't fresh beginnings be possible; why shouldn't weeds fly and trees be uprooted?

"Increase our faith," they ask Jesus. "If your faith were the size of a mustard seed ..." he replies.

Once again, Sister Macrina gets it right as she prays:

O God
help me
to believe
the truth about myself
no matter
how beautiful it is!

The wonder of faith—now the wonder of being faithful.

In the parable, slavery is a very dramatic, negative expression of the more positive biblical value of covenant fidelity. In covenant relationships such as marriage or friendship, generosity, even selflessness, is exercised for its own sake, simply because it's right and inherently good, not because there are "thank you's" or external rewards … quite a challenge for those whose faith is the size of a mustard seed!

Here in this parish, I have seen so many examples of this! A wife who is well into her eighties cares for her husband who has Alzheimer's disease. She gets no thanks or even much acknowledgment from him anymore. She is simply doing what is right and finding herself in that, keeping her promises, honouring her commitment. Her life lived in faith is one of utmost fidelity and a deeply rooted sense of duty embraced in love. In living that love, she experiences well-being and security, a peace that no one can take from her.

Unflattering as the term "slave" may be, Jesus' use of it forces us to reflect on a crucial aspect of our relationship with God and with all of life. When we are at our best as human persons, we are not concerned primarily with being praised, rewarded or promoted. We are simply finding and fulfilling ourselves by being what we are as human beings and acting in accordance with who we are: not masters, but servants.

O God
help me
to believe
the truth about myself
no matter
how beautiful it is!

Can you see the connection between having faith and being faithful?

Most of us are conscious of any number of missteps; we are conscious that we have not always been faithful. Yet the failed relationships and the brokenness that we may have experienced or even caused serve, however painfully, to underline the profoundly human values of duty and fidelity, and to invite us again to seek values that truly endure.

Although Luke probably never intended it, the flying tree and the slave can be good partners.

More Than Skin Deep

Twenty-eighth Sunday in Ordinary Time

2 Kings 5.14–17
Psalm 98
2 Timothy 2.8–13
Luke 17.11–19

I had a delightful experience with the Grade 4 class over at St. Daniel's School just before Thanksgiving. The miracle story of the ten lepers was chosen, appropriately enough, as the gospel for their Thanksgiving liturgy. Few of the children knew what leprosy was so we started talking about other communicable diseases that affect the skin, diseases they might know about from their experience.

Forgetting about the modern vaccine, I started describing my experience with measles as a child about their age. I had had it at Christmas time and didn't even get to miss any school. None of them had ever had measles. Chicken pox was another matter. They all had experience with chicken pox and knew how it could spread through their class and circle of friends. They knew how catching it was.

We discussed that leprosy was a much worse disease than chicken pox, and that moreover, it never got better, just worse. People who had leprosy would have to leave home and live by themselves outside of the towns. They would even have to shout "Unclean!" to anyone who came near to protect them from the disease. We got off track trying to decide how these people would get anything to eat or have clean clothes to wear. One boy wanted to know more about "flesh-eating" disease, which he knew almost took the life of Quebec premier Lucien Bouchard.

With these preliminaries over, the stage was set for the story of the ten lepers. At Jesus' word, the ten were made clean *en route* to their mandatory examination by the priests. Only one, a Samaritan, came back to offer thanks to God. (Our discussion of Jewish–Samaritan relations and thinking about foreigners would come later.)

When asked about why the other nine didn't come back, there were two responses. (The children had obviously been listening very carefully.)

• They were just too excited! They had been so homesick! They couldn't wait to get home to their families!

• Jesus told them to go and show themselves to the priests. They were just doing what they were told. They were being obedient.

In the minds of these children, the nine lepers were by no means bad people. They were just human. These lepers acted as the children pictured themselves acting in a similar situation, wanting to get home and playing by the rules.

The nine cured lepers on their way to the temple had good reason both to be excited and to follow the rules. They knew that there was much more to it than just having nice skin again. To be cured involved readmission to the life of their community, freedom for social inter-action regained, and ritual purity for public worship restored. Delighted with their new freedom, they were anxious to do all that was required to be reintegrated into society. In Jesus' mind, however, something was missing. So focused on themselves and on the world to which they were returning were they that they forgot the Author of Life and Freedom.

The former leper who did return was a Samaritan, a foreigner. He would not have been trained in Jewish law and custom, would have had little interest in showing himself to the priests, and would probably have been given a poor reception at the temple had he tried going there. In typical Lucan fashion, there is virtue in this outsider's dis-obedience that cuts through certain rules and external expectations to the heart of the matter ... another "good Samaritan."

The children did get talking about foreigners, immigrants and refugees on the road to becoming "new Canadians," some of whom were in their school. Two sisters from Romania, whose names were hard to pronounce, were only now preparing for First Communion, although they were in Grades 3 and 5. When they were in Grade 2 in Romania, they wouldn't have been allowed to do so. I told them about a Chinese lady who had come to the 11:00 Mass every Sunday for ten years before she felt free to ask for baptism. We all agreed that the experience of these people was quite different from ours and that their presence among us makes us stop and think.

The eucharistic prayer every Sunday begins with an invitation to thanksgiving: "Let us give thanks to the Lord our God." You will respond: "It is right to give him thanks and praise." In the prayer chosen for today, I will continue: "Father... it is truly right that we should always and everywhere give you thanks and praise....You have no need of our praise. *Our desire to thank you is itself a gift.* Our prayer of thanksgiving adds nothing to your greatness, but *makes us grow in grace.*"

The liturgy's call to praise and thanksgiving is an invitation to live in the real world, to receive and cherish our lives and the whole of creation as a gift from a loving God, to rejoice together in this gift that we are called to share, to live in grace and truth.

"Let us give thanks to the Lord, our God." "It is right to give him thanks and praise."

Howling Before God
and the World

Twenty-ninth Sunday in Ordinary Time

Exodus 17.8–13
Psalm 121
2 Timothy 3.14–4.2
Luke 18.1–8

Only those who are or have been truly desperate can fully appreciate the situation of the poor widow, or even of Moses. For the rest of us, crying out day and night, or sitting on a stone with weary arms raised in prayer, is simply not our experience. It is, however, their faith that stands to challenge and invite our own to grow. The experience of Moses and people like the poor widow serves as what classical theology calls "motives of credibility."

Some of the images of God that are presented in both Jewish and Christian scriptures are startling, even shocking, if we stop to consider them carefully. What kind of God would let the Hebrews win only if their leader had his hands in the air? Or who could dare compare God with an unjust judge who can ultimately be swayed to justice only by the nuisance created by a stubborn old woman who presumably should know her place and stay there?

The situation for poor Moses couldn't have been more desperate. The Book of Exodus tells us how the people are surviving their journey through the Negev desert with only heavenly manna as food. So, thirsty, they panicked and rioted, but, with the staff of God that opened the sea in his hand, Moses struck a rock and created a spring. Now they face another crisis: a desert tribe is attacking. "We're just passing through," the people must have thought. "Why can't they let us alone?"

195

Moses knows from hard experience that it is not his busy hands that rescue his people. With staff in hand, his two hands are raised to the heavens in prayer. What a picture! Night and day… Moses sitting on a rock supported by Aaron on one side and Hur on the other. I like to think that the Israelites saw Moses up there praying, or at least knew that he was there with outstretched arms, and that his presence and prayer strengthened them in battle.

Jesus' parable of the desperate widow has a very realistic flavour. In a traditionally male-dominated society, she would have had little influence. In trying to get a judge to even look at her case, her only resource was sheer relentlessness. She would not let up. She would not be put off yet again.

"When he comes, will the Son of Man find this kind of faith on the earth?" Jesus asks rhetorically as he concludes the parable.

Surely the parable is about prayer, but it's about more than prayer. It's about faith, about a way of being in the world and recognizing your place in the world. It's about living and acting with the kind of intensity and passion we see in both Moses and the widow. Just knowing that such people are around can inspire and strengthen our own commitment to justice. God listens to voices such as these, and so do we.

Betty Williams, the 1977 Nobel Peace Prize laureate from Northern Ireland, offers a wonderful example of someone who is prayerful in this way. She stands with hands outstretched before God and the world, voice raised before God and the world.

She tells about how she witnessed the bombing death of children one afternoon. A little girl died in her arms. The force of the bomb had severed the girl's legs and blown them across the street from where she held the bleeding child. Williams went home in shock and despair. Later that night, when the shock had worn off, the full impact of what she had seen struck her. She stepped outside her door and screamed into the night. Shouting at both God and the world, she moved from house to house, pounding on doors that could easily have opened with weapons pointing at her face. "What kind of people have we become, that children are blown to bits on our streets?" she howled. Within hours the town was awake and 16,000 signatures were on petitions for peace.

Betty Williams is Moses with his hands raised between heaven and earth in prayer and protest: the staff of God is lifted up once again; the troops are being rallied once again. Once again the widow is making her case in a world that seems to have neither fear of God nor respect for humanity.

Psalm 121, which we sang today, assures us that the Lord hears and answers this kind of prayer and this kind of pray-er.

I lift up my eyes to the hills—
from where will my help come?
My help comes from the Lord,
who made heaven and earth.

The Lord will keep you from all evil;
he will keep your life.
The Lord will keep your going out and your coming in
from this time on and forevermore.

Liberation from Suffocating Virtue

Thirtieth Sunday in Ordinary Time

Sirach 35.15-17, 20-22
Psalm 34
2 Timothy 4.6-8, 16-18
Luke 18.9-14

"Jesus told this parable to some who trusted in themselves that they were righteous, and regarded others with contempt." We just heard that parable, the story about the Pharisee and the tax collector.

In her wonderful book *In Search of Belief* (Liguori, MO: Liguori/Triumph, 1999, p. 184), Joan Chittister offers another parable for our consideration. Her book is less a commentary on the Apostles' Creed and more a reformulation of its content, giving the classic text a freshness and renewal. Her parable is found in the chapter "The Forgiveness of Sin." She writes:

> The person telling the story thought it was funny. To be polite, if nothing else, I managed one of those wan anemic smiles that signal the mannered responses we make when we want to be kind but honest at the same time. In this case, what was supposed to be funny, I took to heart.
>
> "Jimmy, the local drunk, fornicator, embezzler, and philanderer dies," the storyteller spluttered, already laughing at the very thought of it. "His wife, a proper lady, wants a nice funeral for him to keep up appearances, if nothing else, so despite the fact that religion meant nothing to Jimmy, she goes to Father Muldowney, the parish priest. 'Please,' she begs the priest, 'I know that Jimmy was a scoundrel and never went to church, but can't you at least bury him and say a kind word

198

over his body?' The priest looked up at the poor, pleading woman and felt sorry for her. 'Oh, all right,' the priest says. 'Bring him to the church and I'll see what I can do.'

The entire city and every one of his relatives down to his third cousins turned up at the funeral to hear what good a priest could possibly think to say about a guy like this. Muldowney took a deep breath, looked over the straining, expectant crowd, thought a minute and said, 'I know Jimmy O'Brien was a drunk, a fornicator, an embezzler, and a philanderer. But next to the rest of his family, this guy was a saint.'

The storyteller moved away laughing too much to realize that I was not. The fact of the matter was that I was too struck at the poignancy of the story to laugh at it. "Isn't it the truth?" I thought to myself. Next to me, everybody on earth is a saint. To whose faults could I possibly point for exoneration of my own?*

"All who exalt themselves will be humbled, but all who humble themselves will be exalted."

A couple of things are at stake here as we put these parables together. The question "To whose faults could I possibly point for the exoneration of my own?" strikes me as crucial here. First of all, using someone else to make me feel good or bad, better or worse, stronger or weaker, is a dead end. As soon as we begin even to compare ourselves with others we're off the mark.

Once in a while when I'm feeling lazy, or there's nothing in the fridge, I walk down to McDonald's for lunch. I pick up the newspaper from the rack on the windowsill and leaf through it, but as I read I overhear conversations going on around me.

"My brother is so much better at tennis than me … I'm gonna quit," a young fellow said to his friend.

"This arthritis is making me feel old. I'm so stiff and creaky. Oh well, I should be thankful that I'm not as bad as Nellie. The poor thing can hardly walk," a lady was saying to her group across the aisle.

---

* Used by permission from *In Search of Belief* by Joan Chittister, copyright ©1999, Liguori Publications, MO 63057, <www.liguori.org>, 1-800-325-9521.

Yes—and so what if your brother's a natural at tennis? So what that Nellie will soon need a walker? Be happy for your brother and know that his tennis playing has nothing to do with yours; help Nellie along, but her condition has nothing to do with your own. If you enjoy tennis, play. Don't let arthritis get the best of you; follow your doctor's advice and keep moving.

From the vantage point of the gospel, comparing ourselves with others, for better or for worse, is *not* what life is all about. Living out of our own strengths, confessing our own sins, rejoicing with those who rejoice, and mourning with those who mourn: this is what life is about.

Unique beings that we are, we have our own set of strengths and weaknesses, our own virtues and our own sins.

Second, and even more importantly for the gospel, is how we understand and experience our relationship with God in all this. In faith, we understand ourselves to be unique manifestations of the wonder of God, made in the divine image.

Recognizing ourselves as a uniquely "mixed bag" puts us in a position not to compare ourselves with others but to communicate— with God in thanksgiving, with them in respect. In the presence of the God of mercy, persons of faith are able to freely and confidently celebrate the limitations of their creaturehood. Before God, persons of faith are reconciled with their own limited reality, not expecting to be or pretending to be more than they are. They are free to be who they are. Conscious not only of their limitations, but of their failures and sins, they say: "God, be merciful to me, a sinner." They say it with confidence, out of their own skin.

Part of the reconciliation that God offers us is the possibility of being reconciled with ourselves, with our own limitations, even with our sinfulness. God's act of reconciliation doesn't just absolve sins, or free people from a sinful mode of existence that makes them slaves to hostility and helplessness. God liberates not only from failure and guilt but also from the suffocating goodness and virtue, represented by the Pharisee in the parable, through which we try to justify ourselves to ourselves and to the world.

God frees us from the ways in which we try to save ourselves and make ourselves acceptable. Jesus' gospel of truth and humility is a free word of grace offered in the face of humanity's floundering efforts to save itself. Out of infinite mercy, God affirms the reality of each person. God affirms what is. God loves. Grace is to be aware of this wonderful truth and to go "down to our homes justified."

On Not Being an Optimist
or a Pessimist

Thirty-first Sunday in Ordinary Time

Wisdom 11.23–12.2
Psalm 145
2 Thessalonians 1.11–2.2
Luke 19.1-10

Zacchaeus was a tax collector and, consequently, a hated man. None of us are fond of paying taxes, but I can't imagine any of us hating those responsible for processing and collecting our annual contributions. Maybe some of us do say that we hate those big deductions on our paycheques, but for the most part we believe that they are necessary, that our contributions will be reasonably well spent, and that our systems are reasonably fair and equitable. Right? Okay. We'll pay as little as possible, and take advantage of every possible deduction, even hunt for loopholes, but we don't hate our government and its agents, do we?

Not so in the Israel of Jesus' time. Never very popular in the ancient world, tax collectors were doubly despised by the Jews: first, because their own countrymen who took these jobs were so devoid of national spirit that they became agents of Roman imperialism, and second, because they were not paid a salary, but a commission of what they collected. It was clearly in the interest of the tax collectors to squeeze everything they could from the people, making relentless and often unfair assessments of people's dues, even deceiving people into paying higher taxes than were owed. That Zacchaeus was very rich says a great deal about how he was discharging his duties.

Jesus was walking through Zacchaeus' hometown, the city of Jericho. He was "passing through" on his way to Jerusalem where his great "passage" would take place. It is noteworthy that this despised little man is so interested in seeing Jesus that he climbs a tree, and even more noteworthy that Jesus, whose "face is set towards Jerusalem," takes the time to so actively "look up to him," seek him out and invite himself to his home for dinner.

Have you seen the film *Gandhi?* If not, it's well worth watching. I may have read about it, but I'm pretty sure it's in the film. At any rate, picture a walk or march that Mahatma Gandhi took with eight of his closest disciples. I find parallels with Jesus' journey to Jerusalem.

In defiance of a government order, they set out on a 200-mile walk to the sea. Gandhi was well known as a staunch opponent of India's stratified society, the caste system. He was also known as an advocate for the "untouchables," those who were members of no caste at all, not even the lowest. One evening, he and his followers arrived at a prosperous village and were given a great welcome. Passing through, much to the chagrin of the village leaders, he found his way outside the village to the hovels of the untouchables. He ate with them; he played with their children; he called them the children of God. Relative to the common belief in reincarnation, he commented that he had no desire to be reborn, but if he were to be reborn, he would like to come back as an untouchable so that he could liberate them, and himself, from within.

Doesn't that sound like Jesus' way of walking, of choosing tables at which to dine? Doesn't it remind you of the incarnation? And what hospitality Zacchaeus gives to Jesus! What a turnaround he makes!

The story is a concise drama of the good news that readiness is all it takes for grace to be activated.

Literature describing the spiritual life sometimes contrasts pessimism with optimism, neither of which are faith postures. Let's take another look at Zacchaeus.

If Zacchaeus were a pessimist, he would have stayed home. He would not have been ready for grace to be activated. He would have been saying to himself: "I'm a sinner. I know what he thinks of me, I'm no good, I've sold out to the Romans, I've betrayed my own kind. I'm the agent of a foreign power and live off commissions paid on the taxes I collect—I sometimes even have to get tough and threaten people to get those taxes. I'm no good, I'm gonna stay home and hide."

If Zacchaeus were an optimist, he would have stayed home. He would not have been ready for grace to be activated. He would have been saying to himself: "One of these days I'll be able to get myself out of this mess. I've been in it for too long and am tired of it. People hate me, but I'm earning a fair income. I know it's a bit cheap— imagine selling myself out to the Romans like this—but one of these days I'll get my act together. I can promise myself that. I'm gonna stay home and do it myself in my own good time."

Do you hear yourself talking to yourself in either of these mono- logues with self? Do you sense in yourself any unreadiness to "leave home"?

Gospel miracles and transformations don't happen with people like this. They happen with people of faith and hope who come out of their caves shrieking, who come out of their villages carrying their dead, who leave their homes, climb a tree, even go out on a limb. Jesus doesn't deal with optimism or pessimism very well, but delights in faith and hope.

In the eucharist, Jesus is not passing by, but inviting himself into your home, "under your roof." Rise and come forward to meet him, waiting in "joyful hope for his coming."

God's Final Judgment

Thirty-second Sunday in Ordinary Time

2 Maccabees 7.1-2, 9-14
Psalm 17
2 Thessalonians 2.16–3.5
Luke 20.27-38

"Some Sadducees, those who say there is no resurrection, came to Jesus and asked him a question." It wasn't really a question, but a sick joke. It's easy to poke fun at or ridicule somebody else's faith or somebody else's way of thinking. Imagine if there were any truth at all in the story: seven brothers die, leaving this woman childless. It's clear that she could not have children. Imagine the humiliation and suffering she would have experienced. What a silly, awful example: "Whose wife will she be in heaven?" It makes the whole idea of resurrection silly, so we can just laugh it off.

The afterlife, heaven, the resurrection: these questions trouble people. We ask them over and over again at different times and stages, and in different life circumstances. I remember a conversation that took place in a family's living room. Lillian had taught with the local school board for many years. I got to know her quite well because she was teaching Grade 2, the First Communion class. She struggled with cancer for a couple of years before her death. When I learned she had died, I went to her home. Her husband and two grown children were at the funeral home making arrangements for the funeral; the school principal and a neighbour were in the living room. The neighbour wanted to talk. She didn't belong to any organized religious group and really didn't believe in the afterlife. "Why should we believe in the afterlife? Lillian was a wonderful person. Do you think she was teaching school and being faithful to her husband to get brownie points from God so that she would be rewarded in the next life, or was she doing that because it was right to do and because she liked doing it? Nobody wants to waste their life or fritter it away, eat, drink and be merry. It's pretty boring after a while. You want your life to be something and to mean something. Whether there is a next life or not doesn't make any difference at all. In fact," she said, "what's this forever and ever? Who wants to go on and on? Why not just pull down the shade?"

There's a legitimacy in what she was saying and what she was thinking, although the principal of the school and I were in no mood to be discussing that sort of thing.

Later her comments made me think of Albert Schweitzer. He started out his remarkable career as an organist, and a Bach specialist. The music of Bach, especially the settings of the chorales, led him to investigate Christianity, which was such an important part of Bach's own mind and soul. Schweitzer, who became a doctor in theology and wrote a book on the quest for the historical Jesus, was never particularly orthodox in his thinking. In his third profession he became a medical doctor and a missionary in Africa, and won a Nobel prize. But throughout his life, he never was sure about very much. He says, "The more we know about God, the less we know about God and what's this heaven business anyway? Life is about living. We just leave the rest of it alone." There's a legitimacy to that. It's okay for Albert Schweitzer. It's okay for Lil. They had good lives; they accomplished something. Their life stood for something.

But what about a young woman who was brutally raped, tortured and murdered? What about her? What about innocent children who suffer the ravages of war? What about them? What about my twenty-one-year-old Uncle Bernard, who was killed in the war, leaving behind his fiancée and elderly parents? My grandfather was blind. What about those seven brothers in the first reading whose young lives are taken by Antiochus, who was making a joke of their commitment to God?

In the centuries just before and after Christ, the resurrection was a very important statement. It was not a carrot at the end of the stick so that if we're good, we'll get to heaven when we die. Rather, it affirmed God's goodness and God's justice, which are greater than anything we can imagine. We put a murderer and rapist behind bars for the rest of his life. That's our justice. But it's not really justice, for justice cannot be done. A Serbian general will be hauled before an international court for war crimes. There is simply no justice that can be done. Nor is justice possible for the little children who were victims of napalm in Cambodia or Vietnam.

The resurrection of the dead affirms that there is another level of life. It affirms that there's a place where God is God, and where God's absolute truth, justice and love will finally be manifested. Karl Marx was wrong when he claimed that this sort of vision is an opiate for people. In fact, it's just the opposite. It energizes. Jesus goes to his death believing absolutely in God's goodness, believing that love is stronger than death. He is energized by this faith to give absolutely everything he is. It doesn't dull his sensitivity to what is going on around him. Rather, it energizes him for death and for life. Christ's resurrection stands as the permanent affirmation and truth of God for all who seek true justice and true peace.

Another example. We always want to know more about heaven than we can. All the silly things about harps and angels just won't do. When Jesus answers the sick joke the Sadducees put to him today, he can't describe the next life—that's not the point. He uses words like "children of God" or "angels." The father of a friend of mine grew up in Quebec City in the 1920s. It was a large family of twelve or thirteen children; the mother died when all the kids were still at home. Their father simply could not manage all those children, so they were placed in strict, very organized, church-sponsored residential schools that were rather narrow in their view. My friend's father was not allowed to think or read a lot of books. When he grew up, he moved to Ottawa and never went back to a church in his whole life. As far as he was concerned, the church, as he had experienced it, was oppressive and narrow.

Still, his wife was a devout Christian whom he respected deeply, and his two girls were brought up in the church. When he died, they brought him to the church for Christian burial. The priest who was presiding at the funeral knew nothing about his story. He just talked about heaven, and the reward of living a good life and being a faithful Christian. It was simply not appropriate! It wasn't true: it didn't represent this man's life at all. As a friend of the family, I was invited to speak at the end of the Mass. I didn't want to contradict the priest, so I spoke a little about this man's life and his values: his integrity and curiosity, the infinite searching that was going on in his life, his loyalty to his wife and his children. I commented, "I think that when he went to sleep for the last time here on earth and woke up in heaven, it was a big, big surprise for him."

The point of heaven, the afterlife, the resurrection, is the absolute affirmation of God's goodness, God's justice, God's truth. Death is not the end. Even a horrifying, brutal rape and murder cannot be a complete, absolute disaster. For believers, there must be something more. There must be another way of affirming life and redeeming, saving, grasping and embracing persons. That's heaven, that's the resurrection; that is God's final judgment. The texts about the resurrection stand as a permanent reminder to all of us that what we see isn't all there is. Our own weak efforts to make a just and wonderful world don't happen in a vacuum. God is at work in these efforts, and in the dying and rising of Jesus, God affirms and guarantees this absolute, final truth.

Steps Towards the End Times

Thirty-third Sunday in Ordinary Time

Malachi 4.1-2
Psalm 98
2 Thessalonians 3.7-12
Luke 21.5-19

But for you who revere my name the sun of righteousness shall rise, with healing in its wings. (Malachi 4.2)

The end of the world is a relative term. The loss of your business could be "the end of the world." The death of your spouse could be "the end of the world." In terms of faith and religion these "ends of the world" can cause deep internal conflict, even despair. What they are depends on how your life is organized, what your priorities are, and what it is about which you feel most deeply.

For the Jewish people, the destruction of the temple was, in a certain way, the end of the world. No longer would their rituals and sacrifices be offered. No longer would they be able to live "normally." Even today there are elements in Judaism that long for the rebuilding of the temple and fully expect that to happen in God's good time.

Most likely, Luke's gospel was completed after the fall of Jerusalem. In today's text he describes Jesus and his disciples admiring its beauty. He seems to foresee its catastrophic destruction. Others likewise foresaw such possibilities. Certain elements in society and religion seemed almost to be tempting Rome's patience with various demonstrations and insurrections. Some even hoped Rome would respond with violence, because that would give God a chance to intervene in favour of his people, bringing about the end of the world as we know it and the definitive breakthrough of God's justice.

There are certain movements even today, perhaps especially associated with "millennium fever," that expect something catastrophic—and *soon*. Jesus discourages this kind of preoccupation: "Beware that you are not led astray," he says, "for many will come in my name and say, 'I am he,' or 'The time is near!' Do not go after them."

The ultimate end is beyond us. It is on the many intermediate ends that attention must be focused, on the difficult and challenging steps along the way.

In the midst of false alarms and premature reactions, the tendency in Luke is to push the final day farther into the future and to redirect attention to that which is more immediate. He invites dealing with the challenges and tensions of the day, chipping away, as it were, at the "old world" to make room for the kingdom of God, the new world of justice, love and peace. When it will definitively break through is not for us to know. It is for us to move in that direction with all our might.

For now, struggle and conflict will be inevitable as an essential component of reaching the goal. Real peace is not easily won; we don't just wish for friendship and understanding; difficult, even painful work has to be done in the meantime. A real and deep coming together is extraordinarily challenging: witness recent seemingly insurmountable obstacles to peace in Northern Ireland, Africa, the Balkans, and the Middle East, not to mention long-standing interpersonal alienation in families, with which we are all too familiar.

This kind of gradual and even painful conversion that takes place along the road to the cross is illustrated in a kind of litany that developed in South Africa for use in reconciliation services and celebrations. It points to something new, the gradual opening up of a new world to replace the old.

> We thought it right to struggle against—we think it right to struggle with
> We thought it right to withstand each other—we think it right to understand each other

We endured our struggle for victory—we endure the struggle
for tolerance
We lived separateness that wounded—we live togetherness
that heals
We believed that we held the truth—we believe that Truth
holds us.

You can almost hear the black preacher at work in those parallel
rhythms.

In the midst of wars, insurrections, earthquakes and famines, "You
will have an opportunity to testify," Jesus says. "I will give you words
and wisdom that none of your opponents will be able to withstand or
contradict."

Even short, intermediate steps towards the end time are not made
easily. The road to Jerusalem is winding and uneven. Certain ways
will have to fall away, and they'll fall hard. Certain presumptions will
have to be overturned; certain temples, however impressive, will have
to collapse. About this, Jesus is very clear, especially as his own personal
end time draws near.

All along the road to Jerusalem, he has broken the grip of traditional piety and the expectations of a stratified society. Every law has
been challenged except that of love. Divine forgiveness has been
proclaimed beyond the structures through which that forgiveness
would ordinarily be exercised. Systems and rituals have been ques-
tioned. All kingdoms have been declared relative to God's.

In word and deed, Jesus announced that the reign of God would
belong to the poor, the meek, the hungry, the dispossessed and the
powerless. Love and readiness to open doors will replace relationships
built on inequality, power and domination.

By his teaching and his personal witness Jesus did not just
announce, but lived this gospel in his own person. It is into this new
world that he invites all who would listen to him and follow. It is
through the cross itself that his resurrection becomes known.

"You will be hated by all because of my name. But not a hair of
your head will perish. By your endurance you will gain your souls."
"Take up your cross, follow me."

More to the Offender than the Offense

Christ the King
(Thirty-fourth Sunday in Ordinary Time)

2 Samuel 5.1-3
Psalm 122
Colossians 1.12-20
Luke 23.35-43

The place where Jesus takes centre stage today is hardly a throne room, at least as throne rooms are pictured in the popular imagination, nourished largely by the happily-ever-after fairy tales of our childhood. We don't see him as a king sitting on a central elevated dais, flanked by the queen and crown prince.

Instead, three crosses are silhouetted against the sky, each bearing the dying body of a criminal. The charges made against them have all been posted. Two are ordinary criminals who have committed ordinary crimes. The other is a crazy man who is being crucified for political and religious reasons. This one is Jesus. The charge posted on his cross is, "This is the King of the Jews." One of the other criminals taunts him: "Are you not the Messiah? Save yourself and us." The other's response to the situation is very different. Let's take another look at what this so-called good thief says.

"Do you not fear God, since you are under the same sentence of condemnation?" In other words, don't you think that you should have other thoughts on your mind than this useless sarcasm directed against your neighbour? "And we indeed have been condemned justly, for we are getting what we deserve for our deeds, but this man has done nothing wrong."

This is the third person who has declared Jesus innocent: Pilate did so, Herod did so, and Pilate did so again, but neither of them would

212

move towards Jesus or even consider his point of view. They were too well positioned in their own worlds.

As we have found so often in this year of Luke that ends today, there is a surprise, a reversal. It is a "fellow criminal, himself hanging on a cross, who says: "Jesus, remember me when you come into your kingdom."

Another surprise! Does Jesus respond: "Today you will be with me in my kingdom"? No. Instead, Jesus says: "Truly I tell you, today you will be with me in Paradise." From his own pain, Jesus reaches out to his crucified neighbour with the hope and promise of paradise. Wherever the word is used in the New Testament, it refers to the garden prepared by God for the first humans. Look back to the beginning of Luke and notice that the genealogy of Jesus goes all the way back to Adam. Today from the cross, the tree of life itself, paradise is being restored by a new Adam, and offered to a criminal.

In offering paradise to the good thief, Jesus, as in all other cases in which he has dealt with sinners throughout the gospel, is not denying the wrong the person has done or the sinfulness of their actions. He is not pretending that nothing had happened, or turning a blind eye to the truth of this man's depravity. His promise of paradise expresses Jesus' ongoing conviction throughout the gospel: no matter what happened in the past, there's more to the offender than the offense. A person is not defined by any action or series of actions. There's more to the person than that, and everywhere in the gospel, it is to any hint of that "more" that Jesus responds with such amazing grace.

The gospel doesn't report how the other thief and the onlookers reacted when Jesus said to the good thief: "Truly I tell you, today you will be with me in Paradise." We can only speculate. Jesus was acting like a king in ways beyond what anyone would expect. His response to his neighbour's request was out of *this* world.

Alice Walker, best known for her novel *The Color Purple,* which was later made into a feature film, shows remarkable sensitivity to the human condition and to the complex ways in which we humans react to and interact with each other. In "Good night, Willie Lee," a shorter piece which first appeared in the *Iowa Review,* she demonstrates that same sensitivity. A woman describes the reaction of her mother to the

death of her father. The relationship was clearly not all that it might
have been over the years.

> Looking down into my father's
> dead face for the last time
> my mother said without
> tears, without smiles
> without regrets
> but with civility
> "Good night, Willie Lee, I'll see you
> in the morning."
> And it was then I knew that the healing
> of all our wounds
> is forgiveness
> that permits a promise
> of our return
> at the end.

quoted in *A Reconciliation Sourcebook*
(Chicago: LTP, 1997), page 191.

She was being a queen in a way no one would expect. Her reaction
was "out of this world."

Like Jesus' word, her word was not pretending that nothing had
happened, but was acknowledging that whatever past offenses there
may have been, *there's more to the offender than the offense*. It is to the
person of her husband himself, not to his offenses, his many offenses,
that she responds before her daughter and before God.

We don't know about the other thief or the crowd in the gospel
story; we do know that the daughter in Alice Walker's story—an
evangelist in her own right, who shares wonderful possibilities with
us as Luke has been doing all year—got it right and wrote it down for
us.

As Year C, the year of Luke, comes to an end today, let's be polite
and thank him. Thanks, Luke, for the Good Samaritan, for the publican in the temple, for the sinner with her tears and her ointment, for
the prodigal son, and for the many unique and wonderful ways in
which you have pulled and tugged at us all year.

Thank you especially today for the good thief and for the hope his presence in paradise offers us all. From your own place there, pray for us, that we may always be open to your reversals and surprises, until we meet you there and finally get it right.

NOVALIS